REDESIGNING VALUE

REDESIGNING VALUE

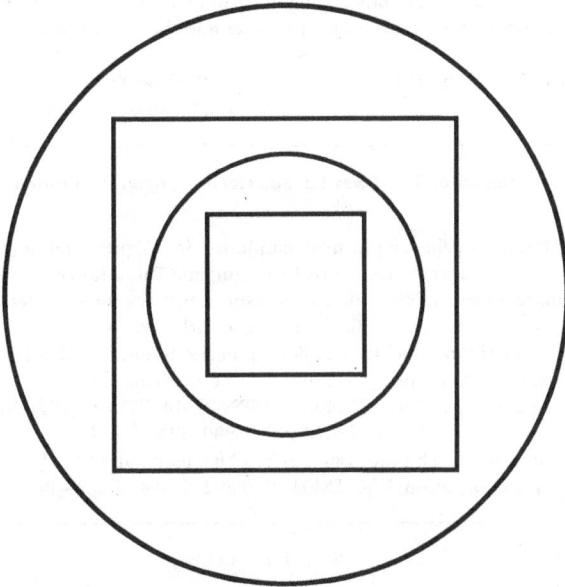

A PRACTICAL MANIFESTO
FOR DESIGNERS AND
ORGANIZATIONS

DAVID DUNNE, CHRIS FERGUSON,
AND PAOLO KORRE

UNIVERSITY OF TORONTO PRESS
Toronto Buffalo London

Rotman-UTP Publishing
An imprint of University of Toronto Press
Toronto Buffalo London
utppublishing.com

ISBN 978-1-4875-5254-1 (cloth)   ISBN 978-1-4875-5519-1 (EPUB)
                                    ISBN 978-1-4875-5389-0 (PDF)

Library and Archives Canada Cataloguing in Publication

Title: Redesigning value : a practical manifesto for designers and organizations /
David Dunne, Chris Ferguson, and Paolo Korre.
Names: Dunne, David, 1953– author | Ferguson, Chris (Lecturer in design), author. |
Korre, Paolo, author.
Description: Includes bibliographical references and index.
Identifiers: Canadiana (print) 20250217139 | Canadiana (ebook) 2025021718X |
ISBN 9781487552541 (cloth) | ISBN 9781487555191 (EPUB) |
ISBN 9781487553890 (PDF)
Subjects: LCSH: Industrial design – Management. | LCSH: Value.
Classification: LCC TS171 .D86 2025 | DDC 745.2 – dc23

Printed in Canada

Cover design: Frontier Design

We wish to acknowledge the land on which the University of Toronto Press
operates. This land is the traditional territory of the Wendat, the Anishnaabeg, the
Haudenosaunee, the Métis, and the Mississaugas of the Credit First Nation.

University of Toronto Press acknowledges the financial support of the Government of
Canada, the Canada Council for the Arts, and the Ontario Arts Council, an agency of
the Government of Ontario, for its publishing activities.

Canada Council   Conseil des Arts
for the Arts   du Canada

ONTARIO ARTS COUNCIL
CONSEIL DES ARTS DE L'ONTARIO

an Ontario government agency
un organisme du gouvernement de l'Ontario

Funded by the   Financé par le
Government   gouvernement
of Canada   du Canada

Canadä

MIX
Paper | Supporting
responsible forestry
FSC® C103567

Contents

Foreword

The dawn of the twenty-first century has ushered in an era of unprecedented challenges. The traditional tools, methods, and frameworks that served us well in the past century now seem inadequate. Consider combating global warming. This is not only a scientific problem to be solved through technological innovation, nor simply a policy challenge to be addressed through legislation. It is a complex web of interconnected issues that spans economics, social behavior, technological capabilities, and political will. It is as much a problem of human behavior as a problem of science.

As David Dunne, Chris Ferguson, and Paolo Korre astutely observe in their groundbreaking book, we find ourselves at a critical juncture where a new type of design problem has emerged. Like global warming, these new challenges are vast and complicated. This is where design serves as a beacon of hope, offering a more nuanced and adaptable approach for navigating through uncertainty. Even though the challenges of today are much more volatile than those of the past, it is worth remembering a few of the social, technological, and economic forces that created challenges in the past and how design progressed to meet the challenges.

The history of design is, to a large extent, the collection of stories about how design modified its body of knowledge (frameworks, methods, and tools) in response to new challenges. Here are a few examples: Streamlining was a visual style that Raymond Loewy, Norman Bel Geddes, and others used to make old products look new. Products looked futuristic even though producers were prevented from making real innovation because of the moribund economy of the Depression and the Second World War. In the booming post-war economy of the 1950s and 1960s, Jay Doblin, Ralph Eckerstrom, Massimo Vignelli, and many others founded Unimark International. It rapidly became the largest design firm in the world. This enabled it to develop specialties in corporate identity and systems design in response to the rampant increase in mergers and global expansion of their clients. In 1973 the OPEC oil embargo caused a severe increase in the production costs of almost all manufacturers. To compensate, manufacturers lowered quality standards causing a decrease in sales and an increase in bankruptcies. Design responded by forming a new specialty called design management. Led by Peter Lawrence in its early years, the Design Management Institute helped connect design to the quality movement.

The particular skills that defined each specialty were clearly different from each other. They had different ways of presenting their work; for example, streamlined drawings of a new product would be unveiled as the work of an artist, while a corporate identity program would stress teamwork and systems. Less apparent than the differences was a common factor in every project: the client. Within fifteen years, however, the client was gone from center of projects, replaced by a new factor: the humans who would use it.

By the late 1980s design faced a transformation of the whole field, not just the creation of new specialties. The transformation was enabled by the confluence of three technologies: embedded computing, flexible manufacturing, and high-speed communication.

Embedding computing in common products like telephones, cameras, and automobiles added functions but made them difficult to use; second, flexible manufacturing enabled more variation in the things a production line produces; and third, high-speed communication and the Web meant most people in the world were connected. Business models changed the activities of work, learning, and play, making them ubiquitous, customized and almost free.

These interactive products and services sparked the specialty called interaction design, while the expansion of consumer choice sparked strategic design. The foresight and energy in both specialties have led us out of the era of industrial design into the era of human-centered design with its user experience frameworks, and methods like day-in-the-life studies, user journeys, scenarios, and personas. Today, human-centered design has become the new normal.

But it is not clear that this is enough. Designers continue to focus on problems as if they were unique, and neglect to build knowledge that strengthens the design field and connects to other fields that make it easier for engineers, economists, and scientists to work with designers. While human-centered design had a highly visible entry by improving the usability of things people touched and the information they needed to understand, it has not paid attention to larger issues that contribute to the major challenges to human well-being. These challenges include knowing the total cost of a product, (including sourcing material and disposing of it at the end of its life); knowing the dangers of environmental hazards where we live, and many others that could be helped by the designer knowing more about design attacking big problems fraught with uncertainty. We can learn how other fields have scaled up. Management, public health, public policy, computer science, and other fields provide examples. If design decides to ignore the large challenges, those working on the challenges will surely ignore design.

This book offers a path for design to build frameworks, methods, and tools that make a difference in how we face seemingly impossible problems. The authors identify six critical "binds" that organizations must untangle to effectively address contemporary challenges. These binds – work style, risk, silos, business model, scope, and epistemology – impede decision-making about what to make and how to proceed in an increasingly complex environment.

What makes this book particularly valuable is its pragmatic approach to implementation. Rather than presenting design as a panacea, the authors acknowledge the real-world constraints and challenges organizations face when attempting to implement more sophisticated problem-solving methodologies.

The framework the authors present is both aspirational and actionable, providing concrete steps organizations can take to enhance their problem-solving capabilities while acknowledging the complexities of organizational change. Innovation, sustainability, complexity, transformation, collaboration, value, and adaptation emerge as the key themes threading through this work.

These concepts serve not just as theoretical constructs but as practical guides for organizations navigating an increasingly complex landscape. The authors' emphasis on these themes reflects a deep understanding of the challenges facing modern organizations and the evolving nature of effective problem-solving.

As we navigate the uncertainties and opportunities of the twenty-first century, the insights and frameworks presented here will prove invaluable for organizations seeking to enhance their relevance in an increasingly uncertain world.

This book is a practical guide for those working to address our most pressing challenges. In the pages that follow, you'll find not just analysis but inspiration – not just theory but practical wisdom drawn from real-world experience. As you engage with these ideas, I encourage you to consider how they might transform your own approach to problem solving and value creation in an age of unprecedented complexity and change.

Patrick Whitney
Distinguished Research Fellow
Brown University School of Public Health
Dean Emeritus
Institute of Design, Illinois Institute of Technology

Acknowledgments

It took a village to produce this book. Between formal interviews, workshops, chats, voice calls, Zoom, Teams, and Google Meet calls, messages, and social media, we benefited enormously from the thoughtful ideas of our colleagues in the design and managerial communities. We were delighted with the energy and enthusiasm our topic generated, and we are extremely grateful for the input we received. These conversations provided essential background material, even if some did not find their way directly into the book.

It would be impossible to thank every individual who contributed here, but we want to single out a few for special mention. Josh Greenhut provided valuable advice as we set off on our writing journey; Jules Maitland at All In Design read our early drafts; Paddy Harrington and Tristan Marantos at Frontier Design did outstanding work on our cover design and graphics; Patrick Whitney wrote a deeply thoughtful foreword. We also owe our deep gratitude to Jennifer DiDomenico, editorial director at University of Toronto Press, for her guidance and helpful suggestions, to Megan Hunt, Leah Connor, and the production and marketing teams, and to the three anonymous reviewers who provided supportive and insightful comments.

Last, but far from least, we owe our deep gratitude to our spouses, Carol Ann, Clarissa, and Sarah, and to our families for their unstinting support and encouragement.

REDESIGNING VALUE

1 Faking Design

The Port Lands are the gritty underbelly of sparkling Toronto. Originally a marshland, they were heavily polluted by industry in the nineteenth century, developed in anticipation of a boom in maritime traffic that never happened; then, in the mid-twentieth century, filled in with waste from the construction of subways and large buildings. By the 2000s, the Port Lands were home to a waste treatment plant, a generating station, a defunct railway line, several industrial plants – and an emerging creative sector, comprising film studios and entertainment venues. They were considered the largest underdeveloped urban space in North America.[1]

In Canada's largest and busiest city, where development land is scarce, the area had long been a question mark. In 2017, it seemed the answer had been found, in the shape of a project that promised not just to develop the area, but to do so in a way that would put Toronto at the forefront of global urban development and turn Canada into a technology hub. What wasn't to like?

Plenty, as it happened.

In 2017, Waterfront Toronto, a hitherto little-known arm of the municipal government, issued a Request for Proposals to develop 12 acres of the 190-acre Port Lands. In October of that year, the project was awarded to an equally obscure, at the time, entity: Sidewalk Labs. As it turned out, Sidewalk Labs was not the urban skunkworks implied by its name, but a subsidiary of tech giant Google's parent company, Alphabet.

Like Google, Sidewalk Labs presented itself as a twenty-first-century corporation at the vanguard of fusing design and data, seamlessly and irresistibly. Sidewalk Labs' proposal was built around blending advanced technology into urban planning, by integrating physical infrastructure, such as buildings, transportation, and utilities. Data was central to the plan, which would involve its collection, and management, as an application programming interface for third-party developers. Designers would then translate data into hitherto unimagined life-enhancing new services.

In 2019, the company issued a 1,500-page document detailing the 160 projects under the plan, such as passive house-inspired buildings with high-performance building envelopes, battery energy storage, rooftop solar panels, pneumatic waste collection, e-bike parking, and charging infrastructure. Beautifully rendered, the proposal was full of designs and images for the city of the future. Of these, 144 were approved by Waterfront Toronto.

Though the 2017 proposal was broadly welcomed – at least by Toronto's chattering classes, and by those who saw the possibility of cool, well-paid, tech jobs – the public mood had shifted by the time the plan emerged. In 2018, Canadian programmer Christopher Wylie had disclosed that his employer, UK-based consultancy Cambridge Analytica, had collected data from Facebook users without their consent, building psychological profiles to be used in political advertising. It was widely believed that this had influenced the UK's Brexit vote in 2016 and the election of Donald

Trump to the White House later that year. Facebook was fined $5 million by the US Federal Trade Commission and paid a further £500,000 to the UK Information Commissioner. Cambridge Analytica filed for bankruptcy in mid-2018.

In a 2016 article in the UK *Financial Times*, historian Yuval Noah Harari warned of "Dataism," a movement akin to a new religion. "In its extreme form," he wrote, "proponents of the Dataist worldview perceive the entire universe as a flow of data, see organisms as little more than biochemical algorithms, and believe that humanity's cosmic vocation is to create an all-encompassing data-processing system – and then merge into it."[2] By 2019, when Sidewalk Labs publicly released its plan, this dystopian view of Dataism was beginning to seem real: Toronto residents could see that Sidewalk Labs could monitor where they went, what they did, whom they interacted with, whom they called; there was even a proposal for a "blood-flow mirror"[3] that would collect data on an individual's state of health and upload it to the internet.

Another major concern was transparency. Though Sidewalk Labs had been clear from the beginning that it aspired to work on the full 190-acre Port Lands, rather than the 12-acre development it had applied for, this larger expansion was initially downplayed. Moreover, Sidewalk Labs hoped to make the area quasi-autonomous, collecting taxes to fund the development of infrastructure and applications. Citizens and activists became deeply concerned, worrying about the expanding role of the private sector in public space. As tech advocate Bianca Wylie wrote, "At what cost and for what reason is a corporation becoming a broker between people and their governments in terms of designing how we live?"[4]

Recognizing the risk of a backlash, Sidewalk Labs retreated to the 12 acres in the original proposal. The company engaged in broad public consultation, in town halls and surveys. It also employed more designerly ways of working, such as co-design at their airy studio adjacent to the Port Lands site. But, as one designer who worked on a project with the team put it, "The purpose of the space wasn't to engage in meaningfully co-creating a better city with citizens, it was to *appear* that they were listening."

The designer continued, "It was a solution looking for a problem. Sidewalk Labs had walls covered in questions about the future and sticky notes. They opened up the space for public events and invited in partners from the community. They presented themselves as a design studio, but it was just a front. When it came to solving problems, the focus was always on their tech, not solving citizens problems. When it came to explaining how they were monetizing the data and technology built on public lands, there was no transparency."

Arguably, Sidewalk Labs *was* a design studio, but a flawed one. The company's timing was certainly unfortunate, but many of the objections could have been avoided had the company engaged fully with the community. "Tech often brings a top-down approach to how decisions are made," said *Globe and Mail* journalist and author of *Sideways: The City Google Couldn't Buy*,[5] Josh O'Kane in an interview.[6] "Cities, when done well, ... are generally bottom-up organizations where people decide what's happening." What the community wanted was not town halls, but true engagement.

From the beginning, the company framed the problem as "how might we use technology to improve cities?", presupposing that the best solution to the city's problems of affordable housing, congestion, and pollution was a technology-based one. No doubt, Sidewalk Labs believed this, but in failing to consult, authentically, with the community to understand how Torontonians themselves viewed their pressing problems, Sidewalk Labs sowed the seeds of its own destruction.

In May 2020, Sidewalk Labs canned the project, citing the COVID pandemic. "As unprecedented economic uncertainty has

Figure 1.1 *Public Consultation at Sidewalk Labs. (Sidewalk Labs)*

set in around the world and in the Toronto real estate market, it has become too difficult to make the 12-acre project financially viable without sacrificing core parts of the plan we had developed," wrote CEO Dan Doctoroff.

"Sidewalk Labs wanted to win so badly that it just kept losing," wrote O'Kane, in his final assessment.[7]

There's plenty of talk about design, but people mean different things by it. For managers – at least, those who subscribe to the traditional paradigm – design is ultimately a way to win: to increase shareholder value, by increasing sales or reducing costs. Designers, on the other hand, typically see their profession as creating value for users and society, with shareholder value a secondary consideration.

Design has been oversold, misinterpreted, and misused to perpetuate an antiquated and destructive business model. Worse still, design has been discredited in the process. Organizations that adopted it as a silver bullet for disruptive innovation were always bound to be disappointed, because the hard truth is that disruptive innovation disrupts the status quo. Such disruption – to internal processes, cultures, and power structures – can be costly, risky, and painful, and many organizations backed away. Their disappointment fed into a narrative among managers that design was yesterday's fad.[8]

Designers know better.[9] The corralling of design in service of shareholder value – in the guise of MBA and executive courses in "business design" and the like – represents a huge, missed opportunity. Properly applied, design has the power to transform experiences on a much wider plane: to help create a world where value takes on a different meaning, making a positive contribution to people, communities, and the planet – rather than focusing only on financial value.

Differing visions of design – as a business tool versus a vehicle for real change – underpin the relationship between managers and designers, leading to frustration on both sides. Managers feel design fails to live up to its promise, while designers feel gaslit by a culture that simultaneously supports and undermines them. As a result, design is misunderstood, trivialized, and hamstrung in organizational life.

We believe both managers and designers can do better. Despite their differences, they increasingly share goals, philosophies, attitudes and aspirations. Both want businesses to make enough profit to flourish, and for those profits to be distributed fairly. Both want to do good things, not just for the corporation, but for people and the planet. We believe that managers and designers *can* collaborate to deal with the most pressing problems in our society by *redesigning value* – creating new kinds of value that put people, communities, and the planet first – if they can find a way to unleash design.

This book is about finding that way. We take a deep dive into the invisible causes, visible impacts, and all-too-visible outcomes of the divide between managers and designers. We look at some ways designers and organizations have bridged the divide, and suggest a path forward to redesign value.

In the remainder of this chapter, we will take a look at the parallel histories of business and design, to show how they got to where they are today.

Redesigning Business[10]

Since the early days of business, those who see it as primarily a vehicle for making its owners rich have faced off against those who believe it should benefit society more broadly.

Andrew Carnegie was born into poverty in 1835, in Dunfermline, Scotland, in a tiny cottage with a shared main room that served as living room, dining room, and bedroom. At the age of 12, he moved to Pittsburgh, Pennsylvania, with his parents. At first, the family struggled to make ends meet – but, through hard work, inventiveness, and organizational talent, he came to dominate the steel industry and become America's richest man by the turn of the twentieth century.

In his memoirs, Carnegie wrote that as a young man, he was very egotistical and greedy.[11] But he changed. After a midlife crisis made him revise his calling, he advocated the principle that a capitalist should not live only to accumulate capital. His 1901 essay "The Gospel of Wealth" argued that the rich should return their surplus wealth "to the mass of their fellows in the forms best calculated to do them lasting good."[12] In stark contrast to many in his time who advocated unrestricted accumulation of wealth, Carnegie saw the inequalities brought about by the relentless pursuit of efficiency.

Yet it is this relentless pursuit that has dominated the business mind since Carnegie's time. In the early twentieth century, Frederick Taylor's "scientific management" sought to improve efficiency through division of labor and piece work – a philosophy that was widely accepted in business and resulted in a massive transfer of power to management from workers.[13] Since the inception of business schools in the early twentieth century, generations of students have been taught that the sole purpose of a business is to enrich its shareholders.

In 1970, economist Milton Friedman wrote a landmark op-ed in the *New York Times Magazine*, "The Social Responsibility of Business Is to Increase Its Profits," arguing that the responsibility of a corporate executive was to "make as much money as possible while conforming to the basic rules of the society."[14] This became the business mantra of the late twentieth century: The business of business is to make money, the business of society is to formulate social policy – and each should keep out of the other's way.

In the 1980s, with Margaret Thatcher in 10 Downing St. and Ronald Reagan in the White House, this pro-business doctrine was reinforced in a wave of privatization and deregulation. Western democracies saw the rise of financialization – the increasing emphasis on financial measurements and institutions – as the powerful focused public and private institutions on efficiency and profit. The cowboy years of the 1990s saw Western society double down on the "winner-take-all" mindset, with the dramatic growth of hedge funds, the explosion of new financial instruments, and the dot-com bubble.

Over the decades, many have bristled against this way of thinking. Renowned economist John Maynard Keynes, for example, is credited with the statement that "Capitalism is the astounding belief that the most wickedest of men will do the most wickedest of things for the greatest good of everyone."[15]

In 2011, business guru Michael Porter became the latest economist to question the capitalist paradigm. In an article in *Harvard Business Review*, Porter and his co-author, Michael Kramer, argued that businesses were "trapped in an outdated approach to value creation ... optimizing short-term financial performance."[16]

The then-prevailing "social responsibility" mindset, they argued, placed societal welfare at the fringes, not the core, of business purpose. Instead, businesses should reconceive the intersection between societal value and corporate performance. How? By creating *shared* value. One of the companies they held up as an exemplar was the Swiss-based food multinational, Nestlé.

Nestlé might seem an odd choice. In the 1970s, you could barely mention the company without the word "boycott" immediately following it. Nestlé aggressively marketed baby formula in developing countries, in the face of scientific evidence that breast milk was the best nutrition source for infants. Its practices led to the company being labelled "baby killers," and, in 1977, to a consumer boycott campaign, first in the US and subsequently in Australia, Canada, New Zealand, and Europe. Nestlé fought back in the courts and in the media, but the boycott continues to the present day. Infant formula is not Nestlé's only controversial issue: The company remains mired in controversy over issues like exacerbating droughts and using child labor in its supply chain.[17]

However, the picture is nuanced. Since the turn of the millennium, Nestlé has developed its "Creating Shared Value" strategy, which arose from a decision to reposition Nestlé as a "nutrition, health and wellness" company. Under CSV, Nestlé would work not only to improve nutrition, but also to conserve water and improve the productivity of its many smallholder farmers and their communities. Over the following decades, the program broadened and deepened, to encompass environmental and community support initiatives. In Canada in 2021, Nestlé invested $460m on initiatives like Black employment, frontline healthcare support during the COVID pandemic, and regenerative cocoa farming practices.[18]

Nestlé was not alone: Food companies like Pepsico, Coca-Cola, Unilever, Danone, and many others invest heavily in communities and sustainability. But at the same time, all these companies have been criticized for exploitative business practices and environmental degradation. Has business really changed, or is this window dressing?

There are indications that the shift is real – at least in some quarters. In 2019, the Business Roundtable, a lobbying organization whose members are CEOs of major US companies, took a radical turn. In its Statement on the Purpose of a Corporation, it argued that

> Businesses play a vital role in the economy by creating jobs, fostering innovation and providing essential goods and services … While each of our individual companies serves its own corporate purpose, *we share a fundamental commitment to all of our stakeholders.*[19] [italics added]

The statement was endorsed by 181 CEOs, each committing to leading their companies for the benefit of *all* stakeholders: not just shareholders, but customers, employees, suppliers, and communities too.

That same year, economist Mark Carney told *The Guardian* that "Firms ignoring the climate crisis will go bankrupt." Carney, a former governor of the Bank of Canada and of the Bank of England, became the UN's special envoy for climate action and finance and, later, prime minister of Canada. He has taken a leading position on climate action and advocated for "green" financing.

What happened to bring about such an about-face in business thinking? To begin with, the dot-com bubble of the early 2000s led many to question the wisdom of investing in "surefire" companies that created only ephemeral – if any – value.

A few years later, the Global Financial Crisis of 2007–8 sent markets and economies spinning. New financial instruments targeted low-income homebuyers, and when the US housing bubble burst, the effect rippled through the economy. Around the world, financial institutions teetered on the brink, and the collapse of Lehman Brothers in the fall of 2008 triggered an international banking crisis.

But the pain was not equally felt by all. The hammer fell heaviest on the people who could least afford it: those whose homes were repossessed and who lost their jobs in the ensuing recession – while, at the same time, bankers continued to enjoy generous bonus plans. According to economists Brian Bell and John Van Reenen,

> Bankers' share of earnings showed no decline between the peak of the financial boom in 2007 and 2011, three years after the global crisis began. Nor did bankers' relative employment position deteriorate over this period.[20]

There had always been dissenters – notably, documentary film-maker Michael Moore and author Naomi Klein – who pointed out the gross inequalities and injustices spawned by a loose regulatory system, driven in turn by the politics of privilege. In 2011, as the gap in wealth between the richest 1 per cent, who own about half the world's wealth, and everyone else became even starker, dissent hit the streets.[21] The Occupy movement protested the control of large corporations and the global financial system held over the world, control that disproportionately benefited the wealthy minority and undermined democracy.

Occupy had a broad influence across society, including among some of the 1 per cent.[22] The NGO Wealth for the Common Good declared itself as *"the 1 per cent for an economy that works for everyone,"* and had a wide network among the wealthy.[23] According to one of its members, Lisa Renstrom, "I grew up believing that capitalism and free enterprise would make the world a better place. The twisted capitalism we practice today has left us with degraded infrastructure, threats to our health, and a shifted climate."[24]

Inequality was also highlighted in French economist Thomas Piketty's landmark book, *Capital in the 21st Century*, in which he traced the history of inequality and argued for a global tax on wealth, to prevent increasing inequality and social unrest.[25] The book became a must-read among economists, business executives, and the public.

As the debate about inequality was heating up, so too was the planet. In many countries around the world, climate change was becoming a major preoccupation with consumers and voters.[26] In 2007, *Harvard Business Review* published a special issue devoted to climate change. "Climate change will affect everything businesses do," argued the editors, "as government efforts to mitigate carbon emissions cause their prices to rise steeply."[27]

The same year, the United Nations argued that public awareness of climate change created a significant opportunity for business.[28]

By 2020, when Mark Carney became the UN's special envoy, the effects of climate change and of government regulation were being felt around the world. Establishment voices, such as *Financial Times* chief economics commentator Martin Wolf and former Rotman School of Management dean Roger Martin, warned that rising inequality and governments' lack of investment in environmental and social good was leading to an ugly fall for democratic capitalism.[29,30]

In response, a swell of citizen-led social movements increased the visibility of pressing social and environmental problems. Widely publicized events such as George Floyd's murder, the sexual assault trial of Harvey Weinstein, and the Canadian Truth and Reconciliation Commission report on abuses and impacts of residential schools uncovered injustices that had previously been hidden from view.[31] From #climatecrisis to #metoo, people became engaged and pressed for change within our private and public institutions. For many, though, the pace of change was far too slow.

In the pages of *Harvard Business Review* and in the statements of business leaders, the world was changing. But on the ground, things seem much the same as ever: Inequality has become ever more outrageous, and many companies continue to pollute as if there is no tomorrow – and arguably, at the rate they are going, there may not be.

Donald Trump's election to the US presidency in 2024 was unquestionably a backward step – but we believe that failure to change is due more to inertia than to malicious intent. Inequality and climate change cannot be solved by grandiose statements: They are the results of a complex global system. Just navigating this system – much less, changing it – demands skills and attributes that do not come naturally to businesses, or governments: an ability to grasp problems quickly and reflect on their meaning; comfort with unfamiliar, uncertain situations; smart, evidence-based speculation; empathy with those most affected by problems.

That's where design can help.

Redesigning Design

"Designers are becoming much more ambitious – perhaps imperialistic – about design thinking," declared *The Economist* in 2013.[32] The comment reflected an adolescent phase in the growth of design in business, government and nonprofits, when designers were adopting an expanded role, but still insecure and conflicted about their contribution. To an extent, this insecurity still exists.

Perhaps the blandest definition of design came from Nobel Laureate Herbert Simon in the 1960s: "Everyone designs who devises courses of action aimed at changing existing situations into preferred ones."[33] The quote shows how hard it is to come up with a convincing definition of design: We are all designers, and we are designing all the time – just as we are all managers, managing all the time.

Along with architect and noted futurist R. Buckminster Fuller, Simon was a thought leader in the "design science decade" of the 1960s, though the desire to "scientize" design goes back to the early part of the twentieth century.[34] Looking to natural sciences, like physics, for inspiration, Simon argued that, while science dealt with understanding existing conditions, design was about transforming things. He characterized design as a type of scientific method, based on technology and rationalism, and aimed at creating new forms, new artifacts, or, more generally, new knowledge.[35] In keeping with the focus on methods and science, Simon coined the term "design thinking"; in practice, this took concrete form as "design methods," still emphasized today at design schools like Chicago's IIT Institute of Design and The Netherlands' TU Delft.

In the 1970s, however, there was a backlash among some designers at what they saw as "design by the numbers." In 1973,

Horst Rittel and Melvin Webber, both professors at University of California, Berkeley, described problems of social policy as "wicked problems."[36] "As distinguished from problems in the natural sciences, which are definable and separable and may have solutions that are findable," they wrote, "the problems of governmental planning – and especially those of social or policy planning – are ill-defined; and they rely upon elusive political judgment for resolution."[37]

By the late 1970s, the idea of scientific design was in decline. One of its erstwhile pioneers, J. Christopher Jones, wrote: "I dislike the machine language, the behaviorism, the continual attempt to fix the whole of life into a logical framework."[38] Philosopher and urban planning professor Donald Schön saw design not as a science, but a "reflective practice," in which the designer responds to the task as it shifts and develops[39] – as messy, problematic situations do.

While scientific design seemed simplistic, Simon's definition of design was deceptively profound: It stated clearly that design was about changing things. Consistency is a virtue in business and governments, and change is often seen as a threat, if at times an unavoidable one. But design is *necessarily and fundamentally* about change.

This divergence between business and design exploded into public consciousness in 1984. It was a tense time, when the forces of technology seemed to be a dark cloud overshadowing humanity. The nuclear arsenals of the United States and the Soviet Union were threatening to obliterate the world many times over; led by vast multinationals, the emerging personal computer felt like the tool of a brutal, inhuman technocracy. At the turn of the year, there was much handwringing about the state of the world, as compared with the dystopia portrayed in George Orwell's classic novel *1984.*

With impeccable timing, Apple fired the first shot in what would become the PC wars, at the January Superbowl: a teaser commercial for its newest computer, the Macintosh.

The ad, directed by Ridley Scott, opens on an unmistakably Orwellian scene, in monotone gray. A phalanx of identically dressed men stares passively at a huge screen, as their dictator announces the "first glorious anniversary of the Information Purification Directives," to ensure unification of thought, an unconquerable weapon against less single-minded enemies. As this is taking place, a nameless woman runs from the back of the theater towards the screen. She brandishes a sledgehammer and wears a white t-shirt bearing the Apple Macintosh logo. She is being chased by masked security guards.

As the dictator reaches the climax of his speech, with "We shall prevail!", the runner hurls the sledgehammer at the screen. With a blinding flash, the screen explodes. A rush of wind engulfs the audience. In a rich baritone, a voiceover announces,

On January 24th, Apple Computer will introduce Macintosh. And you'll see why 1984 won't be like *1984.*

The screen fades to black, and the rainbow Apple logo appears.[40]

The symbolism was lost on nobody. The dictator was the behemoth IBM; the running woman, Apple, the revolutionary upstart. Apple was heralding a new era in computer design, in which user experience came first. IBM's tyrannical technocracy was a thing of the past.

The Apple 1984 commercial was shown only once on network TV, but its impact lasted for decades. Inside Apple, design was fundamental: Design, marketing, and technology all worked hand in hand on the core offering, not just aesthetics. As Steve Jobs famously commented, "Design is not just what it looks like and feels like. Design is how it works."[41]

As Apple confronted IBM, many designers adopted the idea of designing for users rather than faceless organizations.[42] In 1988, in *The Design of Everyday Things*, psychologist Donald Norman argued for more thought to be given to user experience in consumer goods, and particularly in technology.[43]

These debates mostly dealt with *how* designers went about their work. However, there was also an interesting shift in underlying assumptions, one that would become significant later on: *what* is actually being designed. While Simon talked about forms, artifacts, and knowledge, Rittel and Webber used the term "design" in the context of poverty programs, model cities, environmental programs, new religions, and many other social problems.

This seemed at odds with traditional thinking. Professional – i.e., trained – designers focused on two types of design: *graphics* (e.g., advertising and package design) and *physical objects* (e.g., architecture and industrial design).

Richard Buchanan, a design professor at Carnegie-Mellon University, however, saw the need for an expanded definition of design, through design thinking, as a liberal art. "The new liberal art of design thinking," he wrote in a classic 1992 paper, "is turning to the modality of *impossibility* ... it points toward something that is often forgotten, that what many people call 'impossible' may actually only be a limitation of imagination That can be overcome by better design thinking."[44]

In 2001, he expanded his thinking by defining the Four Orders of Design (see Figure 1.2).

"It is certainly important," he argued in his classic paper, "Design Research and the New Learning,"[45] "that designers know how to create visual symbols for communication and how to construct

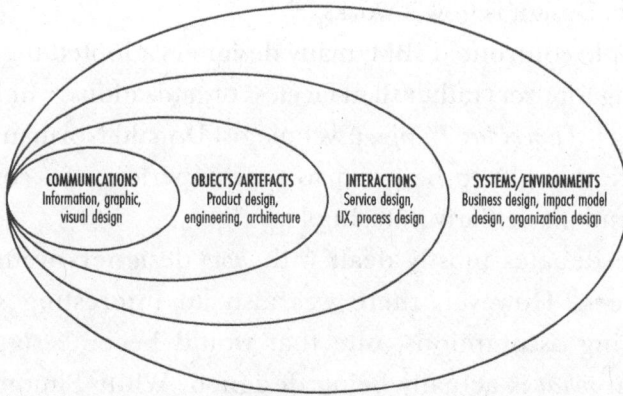

Figure 1.2 *The Four Orders of Design. (Adapted from Buchanan, 2001)*

physical artifacts, but unless these become part of the *living experience* of human beings, sustaining them in the performance of their own actions and experiences, visual symbols and things have no value or significant meaning" [italics added]. Design could not operate in a vacuum; and once you start becoming part of the living experience of human beings, you begin to realize that you need a way of creating lasting value, not just adding more "stuff," or more advertising for that stuff.

To design products and graphics was, from the user's perspective, to design *actions*. Buchanan argued for design to include such actions. In this way of thinking, to design a website is to design the user's inter*action* with it, and to do that well, you have to understand the user's lived experience – how, why, and in what context the website was being used. Design research sought to add this contextual understanding, and this in turn sparked reflection: By venturing outside the walls of their organization, designers often encountered tensions between users' values and organizations' increasingly financialized focus.

In addition, Buchanan argued that the design of *environments* was fundamental to any contemporary way of thinking about design. "The focus is no longer on material systems – systems of 'things,'" he claimed, "but on human systems, the integration of information, physical artifacts, and interactions in environments of living, working, playing, and learning."[46]

Including actions and environments – alternatively, experiences and human systems – in the domain of design was a massive shift. Designers had always concerned themselves with the people who used their designs, and the context within which they were used. But, by the twenty-first century, people, communities, and systems of all kinds – health systems, business systems, pollution, climate change – were not just things you should take into account as you design the next cool smartphone, but fundamental to human survival. They became the subject matter of design itself. Designers had moved beyond the realm of designing "toasters and posters" to design at higher orders.

The era of strategic design was born. Experiences and environments could not be designed in isolation: You had to consider their impact much more broadly, on other products, on services, on the organization and its competitors and collaborators, and on social systems. The designer, formerly relegated to making and drawing, had to become a strategist.

"Strategic designers play multiple roles," wrote Liu and de Bont in 2017.[47] "They are the catalysts and analysts of strategic analysis, the synthesizers and evaluators of strategic decisions and the implementers of strategies." That same year, at the Montreal World Design Summit, UNESCO issued the Montreal Design Declaration, positioning design as not only the process for creating spatial, visual, and experiential environments, but as a driver of innovation, an agent for sustainable solutions, an expression of culture, a means of adding value to technology, facilitating change, introducing intelligence to cities, addressing technology and managing risk, and fostering development of SMEs and the creative industries. Again, it's hard to think of anything – at least anything worth doing – that does *not* fall under this definition: If design can't save the world, nothing will.

While the UNESCO definition took a broad social focus on design, its potential was not lost on the business community. Tim Brown, CEO of design firm IDEO, declared that "Design thinking is a human-centered approach to innovation that draws from the designer's toolkit to integrate the needs of people, the possibilities of technology, *and the requirements for business success*" [italics added].[48] Similarly, business school Dean Roger Martin argued that it was "the next competitive advantage."[49]

This idea appealed to the managerial class. In *Managing as Designing*, business professors Richard Boland and Fred Collopy argued that managers should act not only as decision makers, but as designers.[50] Many in the business audience took from this that, given the right tools, anyone could "do design" to innovate and solve wicked problems. The term "design thinking," long established in the design community, was adopted to suggest that anyone could *think* like a designer without actually *being* one.[51]

With the popularization of design in the business community, misconceptions have commoditized it, turning it into a business tool, a way to tweak rather than disrupt; to extract more, rather than create real value for people, society and the earth – to keep the train running ever faster on the same track, rather than question where the track is leading us.

This is not to argue that viability is an irrelevant consideration in design. Quite the opposite: If designers fail to consider the financial viability of their work and the operations of the organization, their creations will never see the light of day. However, when financial viability is used as the sole pretext for evaluating design ideas, it may hide other, unstated, concerns: disruption to the status quo, short-term thinking, or undue caution.

Designers have watched this commoditization of design take place, and many have expressed alarm. Some have not reacted constructively: Interested primarily in people and creativity, and lacking finesse and strategic skills, they can come across as naïve, righteous prima donnas.

In spite of all this, we believe that design has real power as a means of approaching strategy – by making sense of ambiguity, being sensitive to context, empathizing with humans, and concretizing abstract ideas. It is on this side of design that both the business community and the design community stand to benefit but are failing to collaborate.

Neither managers nor designers have caught up with the potential of strategic design. Stuck in an outdated concept of design, businesses relegate it to making and drawing, while designers typically lack the tools and conceptual skill to contribute meaningfully to strategy.

Redesigning Value

Designers and managers want the same thing: a sustainable world where humans can flourish – but too often fail to connect. Though they have been on converging paths for decades, they repeatedly misconstrue each other's intent, misunderstand what the other needs, and communicate badly. Sometimes, they retreat into caricatures of each other: the diva designer, the rapacious robber baron, or the boring accountant. More often, they become prisoners of misconceptions that arise from their different backgrounds and training, and that trap them in unproductive ways of thinking.

In organizations, these show up as what we call *double binds*, or conflicting messages, a term defined by psychologist Gregory Bateson: "A situation in which a person is caught between two conflicting demands or expectations, with no way to resolve or escape from the dilemma, often resulting in psychological distress or dysfunction."[52] Bateson, a researcher in family therapy, argued that every message has a *report* and a *command* function, representing the explicit, verbal message and the underlying message. He argued that psychological problems tended to occur in families where report and command functions were inconsistent – in other words, when the explicit message and the underlying message differed. Double binds arose from these inconsistencies; in families, they are associated with schizophrenic disorders.[53]

Double binds can be useful in design, when it comes to understanding how a system sends contradictory messages to its stakeholders. According to design theorist Dan Lockton, contradictions may occur when different levels of the system frame the problem differently. Uncovering double binds as from the perspectives of different stakeholders can point the way to solutions, or at least to useful ways to map the system from these diverse perspectives.[54]

Designers in organizations are constantly exposed to destructive double binds. On the one hand, design is explicitly supported and even nurtured, while on the other, the conditions, culture, and implicit beliefs of organizations block and undermine design, preventing it from achieving its potential. In our research, we identified six: the Workstyle bind, the Risk bind, the Silo bind, the Business Model bind, the Scope bind, and the Epistemology bind.

The first three of these, the Workstyle, Risk, and Silo binds, are about day-to-day obstacles faced by designers, as a result of cultural and structural factors in organizations. The Business Model bind deals with the underlying model of traditional business, one of extraction rather than co-creation of value. The Scope bind concerns the results of these four binds: the trivialization and commoditization of design in organizations. The sixth, the Epistemology bind, goes deeper, into differences between managers' and designers' underlying ways of thinking, what they value, and what they view as legitimate knowledge.

We should stress that these double binds result from *differences* between managers and designers: They are not the result of deception, lack of commitment, or hostility to design. Inevitably, too, when we talk broadly about managers and designers, our generalizations mask a wide range of individual behavior on both sides, from the dysfunctional to the heroic, and all shades in between.

Neither managers nor designers are specifically to blame for the double binds – yet both can do better. In each chapter, we identify practices that managers and designers have developed that can help mitigate the problems we identify. Our final chapter, "Value, Redesigned" points the way to a different future, by outlining some broad principles arising from the insights we developed in the course of our research. These can serve as a benchmark for planning design initiatives in organizations to fulfill design's potential.

This book is for both designers who want a fulfilling design practice that makes a difference in the world, and managers, who want to create unique, sustainable value for their stakeholders. We wrote this because we believe that the route to a better world lies in untying double binds, for everyone's benefit. By doing so, we can be more sustainable, more concerned with the impact of our work on humans, more willing to embrace ambiguity, more pragmatic – *and* financially viable. Together, we can redesign value.

In different ways, each of the authors is a strategic designer, bringing decades of design and business expertise to the ideas you will read in this book. David is a business professor who has been researching, practicing, and teaching design for 20 years; Chris is founder of a globally recognized design studio, and a design professor; and Paolo is a classically trained designer with deep expertise in design within healthcare organizations. In boxes in later chapters, we will discuss our individual journeys that have led us to write this book.

Because we work primarily in, or with, the American and Canadian corporate sectors, many of the stories we tell relate to these sectors; we have also worked extensively in healthcare, and some of our most compelling examples come from that sector. However, having trained, practiced, and conducted our research for this book around the world, we believe the underlying principles we discuss are broadly applicable.

For this book, we consulted over 100 designers and innovation managers about their experiences, the obstacles they have faced, and the ways they have overcome these obstacles. Many of the stories they told us will be cringingly familiar to readers who have experienced double binds in their own organizations. You will find here not just an analysis of the double binds, why they arise, and how they are manifested – but solutions that have been tried, tested, and found successful, and a pathway to a better future.

The failure of Sidewalk Labs was a failure of pseudo-design, a distorted corporate version of design that primarily served the company, not the community. But true partnership between designers and managers can transform strategy and make the world smarter, cleaner, and more egalitarian – the kind of value we *all* care about. When you redesign value, everybody wins.

2 The Workstyle Bind

Design has been oversold as an easy process anyone can follow to get miraculous results. But design is neither easy nor miraculous. Nor is it just a process: It is an entirely different way of thinking and working, but one that does not fit comfortably within the routines of many organizations. Failure to provide the working conditions for good design leads to underperformance, and ultimately to the failure of design.

In the winter of 2011, the Service Design Network hosted its annual Global Conference in Berlin. Several hundred designers from around the world gathered to attend talks, participate in workshops, and participate in the annual award celebration. On the opening morning, there was a buzz of excitement as attendees shuffled into a crowded hall at the University of Berlin.

The first presentation of the day was by two young designers working for a large European bank on credit card service. Visibly nervous in the presence of a large audience of their peers, the pair shared their story of how they redesigned the sign-up portal where people applied for credit cards. They walked through the process they had followed, showing visual mock-ups and iterations of a newly developed website. At the climax of their talk, they proclaimed the result: The new design had helped increase business for their client by making it easier for people to sign up for new credit cards. Looking relieved that they had gotten through the presentation, they awaited questions.

One of the leaders of the conference, a legendary designer and leader within the service design community, strode up to the microphone. She was blunt. "I don't see how this is a service design project," she said. You could feel the presenters' embarrassment, as they shifted uncomfortably on stage. They seemed baffled. Stammering, one of the team defended their work by outlining the process they had followed: They had conducted user research, ideated, prototyped, and iterated on their solution. They had faithfully followed the design process that had been widely adopted by the business community, which yielded a net increase to the business targets the bank had set. Wasn't this design?

"You made a website to push credit cards," retorted the community leader. "You didn't touch the service experience. That is not good design."

The interaction highlighted a tension at the heart of design: whether the primary role of design is to deliver short-term results for business owners – increased sales or reduced costs – or a broader one, to create better experiences for users and society.

To conduct their work effectively, designers need to do more than follow the process. They need to deviate from business-as-usual and follow a very different path, one that regularly runs up against organizational ways of working. This tension, which arises from a misunderstanding of the true role of design, underlies the Workstyle bind.

The Workstyle Bind

Organizational leaders promote design thinking but implicitly assume that it will fit readily into existing work patterns. They do not provide conditions that support the unique workstyle that enables good design. In the Workstyle bind, designers find themselves confused; you want design, but you don't want me to work like a designer. The result is a linear form of design that may serve short-term corporate interests, but falls short in advancing the interests of users, communities, or the planet.

How the Workstyle Bind Is Experienced

Design relies on exploration, encouraging emergence, and being open to ideas, which means letting go of some control. This flies in the face of traditional management cultures that value control and predictability. Designers encounter the Workstyle bind when they meet resistance to their optimism, to finding safe psychological and physical spaces, to working physically, and to exercising the craft of design.

Optimism in Exploration

Designers cultivate a habit of putting aside ideas and committing to any particular direction until they have established insight into the experiences and needs of users and stakeholders. Only then can the problem be well defined. This does not mean designers don't have ideas – rather, as ideas emerge, they are put aside in a parking lot, to avoid biasing the team, who may try to find problems that match the solution.

Managers who have not cultivated this practice tend to be impatient and expect the design team to pre-commit to a direction or type of solution. Bruno Silva, former design leader at Mount Sinai Hospital in New York, was often at odds with other hospital leaders when scoping a project. He would receive a request to design an app, or a portal to improve a patient or provider experience, to which he would explain that while an app *might* be a solution, it's important to go through a discovery process first to understand people's needs. His response would be met with blank stares and "yes, but what are you designing?" or "how do you not know what it is?"

At the outset of a project, designers set off without knowing exactly where they will end up or what the outcome will be. This demands confidence that, through an exploratory process, the team will identify clear insights, and will be able to use these to help generate valuable ideas. Managers who have little or no experience with the design approach generally do not have the same confidence; from their perspective it is simply not reasonable to invest the time and resources based only on faith that an unknown outcome will be reached.

Finding Safe Psychological Space

Designers often have trouble shielding insights and ideas from premature criticism.

A common requirement of design workshops and collaborative exercises is the deliberate suspension of judgment. Ideation and sensemaking workshops usually have participation guidelines, at the top of which is to suspend judgment, or to follow improv rules that participants respond to other's ideas with "yes, and ..." instead of "no, but ..." The purpose of these guidelines is to make participants feel safe in suggesting ideas, and to protect fragile, early-stage concepts from premature termination.

Leaders and managers regularly violate these guidelines – with the result that many insights, and great ideas, are lost. In one case in our own experience, a design team was facilitating a workshop within a large insurance company. The team reviewed data gathered from qualitative interviews, verbatim comments from surveys, and stories from member-service agents. As participants were starting to come to a consensus around themes, the vice president to whom the team reported dropped in and listened to the emerging insights.

One of the themes was lack of plain language in the company's communications. When the VP heard this, she slammed the team's work. Communication wasn't an issue for member experience, she argued, and the team should be more focused on the member. To the team, it felt as if they had been completely undermined.

Silence descended on the room. After she left, participants were unwilling to share any thoughts beyond the obvious. Later, one of the organizers said, "We spent the next four hours trying to recover and build back the trust with the team, and the comfort that would allow them to share."

Chris McCarthy, founder of the Innovation Learning Network and former lead of the Kaiser Permanente Innovation practice, said that one of the most important roles he plays is to manage the exposure of his team to leaders. "The questions they ask are cutting, and the ideas are so fragile. With the wrong mindset, leaders can be very destructive." McCarthy was very mindful about the appropriate times and circumstances to invite leaders and other collaborators to participate.

When individuals feel at risk of being judged, they retreat to safe ideas. In 2012, Google launched Project Aristotle,[1] a study of over 180 teams within its organization, to identify the characteristics of a high performing team.[2] The most crucial factor, the study found, is psychological safety. Jen Recknagel, director of NORC Institute and OpenLab at Toronto's University Health Network, agrees. "Creating that kind of space," she said, "helps develop interesting ideas. Whereas if everyone is tight, and when people are worried about being wrong, they freeze up, they hold back."

The Value of Walls and Stickies

Organizations that want to encourage collaborative design work often overlook a critical element in their physical environments: wall space for people to work together.

It may seem trivial, but wall space is important to design. Why? It enables a collaborative and visual way of working. To many, it appears that designers are obsessed with sticky notes: Any designer will tell you they are constantly being told they should invest in 3M, because of all the Post-Its™ they use. Such comments, if tedious, are light-hearted responses to the distinctiveness of the design workstyle – but sticky notes are actually important, for a number of reasons.

John Pipino, affectionately known as Pip to his colleagues at Doblin, talked about the importance of the sticky note. "When everybody has Post-Its™ and a marker, and there's a poster and a place to put stuff," he said, "everyone is simultaneously allowed to place their thoughts into play in a balanced, perhaps even egalitarian, way. That changes the dynamic of how people work together right away."

By contrast, in traditional meetings, a central presenter stands at the podium or, in virtual meetings, is in control of presenter mode. The presenter directs the narrative, moderating the flow of information and ideas. Meetings tend to be didactic, linear, and hierarchical: Participants are acculturated to offer thoughts and ideas only when called upon. Even in meetings that are intended to encourage discussion, hierarchies and norms of exchange limit the free flow of ideas.

Second, sticky notes facilitate rapid thought experiments, and iteration on ideas. You must edit your stuff until it's right," added Pipino. "Post-Its™ allow us to move things around ... so these kinds of tools allow us to recast our thinking, until we feel it's right." Participants are not afraid to postulate different ways of organizing research findings or new ideas, because they can very easily undo or change their thinking.

A third aspect of sticky notes is that it helps teams work with a lot of data to synthesize insights. Neuroscientists have done experiments to show that, while the brain's capacity is in the realm of 2.5 petabytes or a million gigabytes, the ability to hold data in its short-term memory, to think about and work with at any given time, is quite limited.[3] Many psychological studies have shown that our short-term memory can hold only a limited number of separate items: The average is about seven, plus or minus two.[4] This is significant when it comes to trying to make sense of complex problems and disparate bits of data.

By capturing data on sticky notes and on whiteboards, workshop participants externalize data and free up their mental capacity to look for patterns.

With more conventional formats, like Word documents and spreadsheets, information is structured in a very linear way, and you can only see so much of it at once, making it difficult to spot patterns and connections between two distant ideas.

Even in a remote work environment, people are still used to communicating, meeting, and exchanging information in traditional ways, through software that does not enable the same visual collaboration. Though they are a critical enabler of design workstyle, designers often run into resistance from workshop participants to working visually with sticky notes, whiteboards, or other visual media.

Walls, and space to move around, are essential. Yet in modern openplan offices, there is no place for sticky notes, and meeting rooms

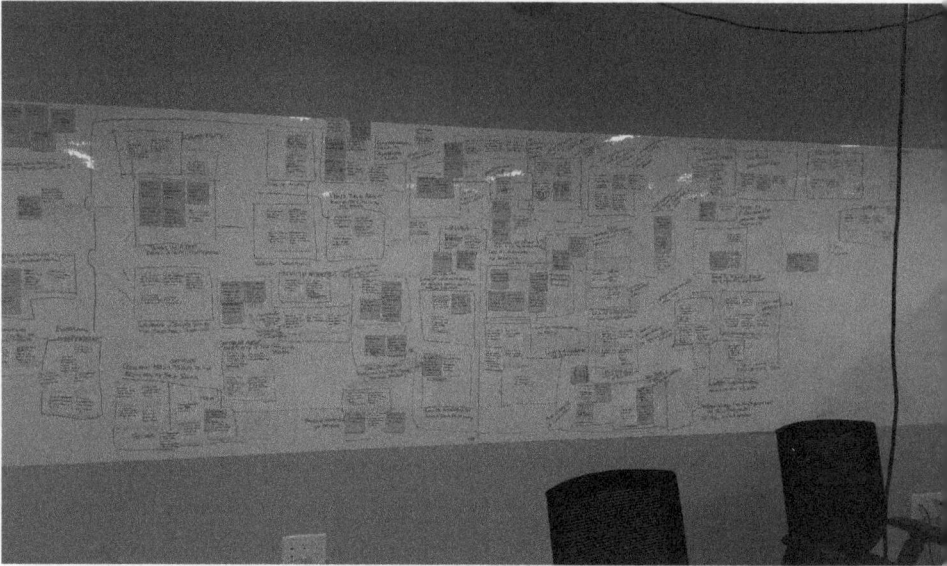

Figure 2.1 *Externalizing data with sticky notes.*

often have a large table that obstructs free flowing work. In addition, meeting rooms are typically used by different teams, so sticky notes cannot be left on the wall till the next design meeting. Minor as these considerations may appear to those unaccustomed to design, they have a significant impact on the quality of design work.

Making to Think

There is real misunderstanding around the role and value of drawing and making. Many managers think of it as an artistic medium and, feeling unskilled, bristle at the idea of having to draw or make things.

Drawing is perhaps the simplest method of prototyping, a way to manifest new ideas and abstract concepts in a way that others can relate and react to. It is much easier for a collaborator, stakeholder, or customer to sense and react to a new idea when it is taken out of an abstract state and made visual. Even something as conceptual as a service or business model can be better communicated and aligned upon as a drawing, turned into a role play, made into a video, or built into a product. Designers place high value on physical representations of ideas, because they allow other people to react and give feedback.

Many designers make a habit of drawing as often as possible: "We have paper and markers in caddies on every single table in this office," said one, "and they're there because [otherwise] we tend to talk, and talk [and] it just disappears into the ether."

In one specific case, a potential client came to a studio with a written proposal for a project that explored the relationships between the different locations of an organization. Said the design leader, Sarah Cantor of Greater Good Studio, "It was really confusing, and everybody was going back and forth, asking him just a ton of questions that [the potential client] couldn't answer." The team tried a different approach: "They just drew it." A network of 70 affiliates, tied to headquarters, was represented by basic shapes and symbols, with arrows between the sites depicting the flow of information between the nodes of the system. What started out as a complicated and abstract description of an organizational structure and business strategy turned into a rudimentary illustration that all could understand. Suddenly, everyone was on the same page, aligning around abstract challenges the organization was trying to tackle: "The client was amazed by what he saw, and how drawing it together helped clarify the thinking and the challenge for the team."

But there is another important benefit in drawing and making: It is an effective way to help teams think. Making can be a form of active inquiry, allowing individuals to explore and experiment with different perspectives and possibilities. For example, sketching can be used to represent unique design concepts or to map out complex systems or relationships.

Drawing and making allow individuals to represent visually, and manipulate, information in ways that can enhance their understanding and generate new insights. They can help communicate ideas, capture observations, explore possibilities, and make connections between different concepts or phenomena. While the drawings themselves help with communication, just through the *act* of drawing, individuals can externalize their thoughts, and define ideas more clearly, surfacing inconsistencies and exposing vagueness. Yet, in the corporate world, physical work like drawing and making are treated with disdain as "play," the business of children, not the serious work of serious people – a mindset that contributes to the trivialization of design.

Intuition and Craft

If anyone can use design methods to practice design, does that mean anyone who does so is a designer? As the opening story to this chapter showed, following the design process does not necessarily mean changing the user experience, nor in itself yield good design. There is still craft in the practice, and good designers have learned to trust and utilize intuition. Yet there is little scope for design intuition in large organizations.

Many designers report that, even where they can lead workshop participants through design methods, the participants often fall short when it comes to making unconventional connections. In one workshop to redesign the recovery journey for stroke patients, notes from research studies on the patient experience were pre-captured on sticky notes, and the participants' objective was to review and discuss the research findings and identify meaningful patterns in the data. One of the groups focused on reviewing and synthesizing data around the challenge of transportation and getting access to the rehabilitation services needed for recovery. The group read and discussed each sticky note, and placed them on a board in clusters, identifying patterns in the research.

But instead of identifying useful patterns around the patient experience, themes like difficulty finding information about public transportation, difficulty in arranging public transportation options and the like, the group ended up classifying types of transportation: public transportation, and private transportation. Despite extra support, facilitation, examples, and direction, the group was just unable to recognize other patterns.

It would be natural to assume that this must have been a result of unclear or insufficient instruction about the exercise, or lack of clear examples. However, this was not an unusual occurrence in this kind of exercise: collaborators just not being able to connect the dots.

A similar issue emerges in generative/ideation sessions, where collaborators are brainstorming new ideas to address a challenge. A design facilitator will prime the participants by helping to immerse them in the data and build empathy towards the end user. The facilitator will then introduce the design challenge; for example, *How might we enable stroke victims to reliably access clinics?* The participants are encouraged to generate as many ideas as they can, before sharing with one another. A good facilitator will use different creative techniques to prompt new ideas, such as Assumption Busting; Design by Analogy; Bad Idea/ Good Idea; SCAMPER, and so on.

Typically, however, participants look to ideas they have seen or heard elsewhere. The prompts matter a lot less than ideas that the participants have already been exposed to.

Professional designers, on the other hand, are much better at connecting the dots: spotting meaningful insights in synthesis workshops and generating many more creative solutions in ideation sessions. Designers nurture and develop the ability to make connections quickly between disparate ideas and bits of data that reveal insights and lead to innovation.

When asked about how to improve, develop, and foster an innovation practice within an organization, McCarthy made it plain: "Hire classically trained designers." Designers, he argued, who have spent time training and learning the craft can recognize patterns and insights, and connect them to valuable new ideas, in ways that others are unable to. As businesses and governments seek to build internal design capacity, it is important to recognize that, while design is an inclusive field, not everybody can be a good designer. While practice and knowledge of design methods are valuable, craftsmanship and intuition are at least as important, if not more so.

Understanding the Workstyle Bind

Many people have been exposed to the concept of design well before they enter the working world. Design and the visual arts are widely considered a practice – often an elitist practice – that relies on the creative whims of an inspired individual. While designers tap into a familiar mental process, it seems to others that it is hidden inside a black box, inaccessible to people who are not naturally creative, or have not nurtured and developed their creativity.

It is seductive to think that with the widespread promotion of design thinking, modern designers and business leaders have found a way to harness the creative potential of design without the risk and unpredictability of traditional creative practices. Paolo's design evolution, discussed in the box, describes how, despite design's rigor, there remains a strong element of intuition and a need to create the conditions that bring it forth.

INTUITION AND METHOD IN DESIGN: PAOLO'S DESIGN EVOLUTION

Paolo's love of art, drawing, and making led him to Toronto's OCAD University, to study industrial design. Though his initial intent was to learn to create furniture and sports equipment, one of his professors challenged him to a bigger vision of design: "Does the world need more designer furniture? Isn't there enough? Isn't there enough waste? Couldn't you use your creative talents to design things people really need, and solve problems that actually matter?"

The question reflected a shift in philosophy at OCADU, consistent with the broader design community's move towards applying design to strategic, social, and environmental issues. While part of the faculty continued to teach traditional product design craft, some had started to try to push in new, more strategic directions.

Project work reflected this shift, becoming more concerned with human experiences and service models than the aesthetics and usability of physical goods. As a result, Paolo gained intuition, and the ability to interpret lofty ideas to develop imaginative products, services, and experiences. But these qualities were tactile and instinctive, and defied explanation.

His graduate studies at the Illinois Institute of Technology, Institute of Design, shifted his direction to one that emphasized the rigor, methodology, and process required to solve complex problems. He vividly remembers his first class, taught by Larry Keeley, co-founder of Doblin, who said, "[When facing a complex problem] if you have the urge to be creative, lie down until the feeling passes." Creativity, Keeley was saying, had a place in design, but with complex problems, it was more important to be consistent, reliable, and systematic.

Paolo learned to communicate the nature of his design practice – not as a black box but as a rigorous process that did not rely on individual creativity or whim. By this time, "design thinking" was being promoted in the business community, and his concept of design was readily accepted.

Yet despite this focus on method and discipline, there were elements that he could not neatly plan or explain. Frequently, he found himself deviating from his plan once he started conducting research. The rigorous process he was telling business partners about was not enough: There still had to be an element of intuition and craft that could only be gained through experience.

After years of practice, Paolo found an equilibrium between the creative and the controlled; he applies structure and method, but today much of his practice focuses on *creating good conditions for human cognition and creativity* – his own and that of his colleagues.

Too often, this unquantifiable aspect of design is overlooked, and as a result businesses fail to establish the conditions for it to flourish. When design is seen as a linear process, its true potential for exploration and breakthrough thinking is lost.

Design Represented as a Process

While inaccurate, the portrayal of design as a process makes sense in a business context. Much of IDEO's[5] and Roger Martin's[6] success in bringing design to the business community came from making a creative methodology accessible to a business audience.

When design was simplified to a series of predictable steps, such as the five-step Stanford d.school process shown in Figure 2.2, it felt familiar to professions that value rationality, control, and predictability, who might otherwise be put off by nonlinearity and iteration. A codified process like this – albeit a misrepresentation of the iterative and tactile nature of design – was much easier to plan for: A road mapped with timelines was much more inviting to collaborators, and consistent with established business planning cycles.

Designers, too, benefited from the illusion of predictability. By having a clear and repeatable process, they could build optimism around their ability to tackle complex problems – when people questioned why things were taking so much time, or seemed off the rails, they could always default to "trust the process."

But boiling design down to a series of predictable steps also meant that design was no longer the exclusive domain of designers; it didn't matter whether you could draw or make, or whether you had an ounce of creativity – you could practice design thinking. As Martin exhorted, "businesspeople have to *become* designers."[7]

Good designers spend years honing their craft. Though businesspeople may learn about design through the many executive courses that are available, understanding design is not the same

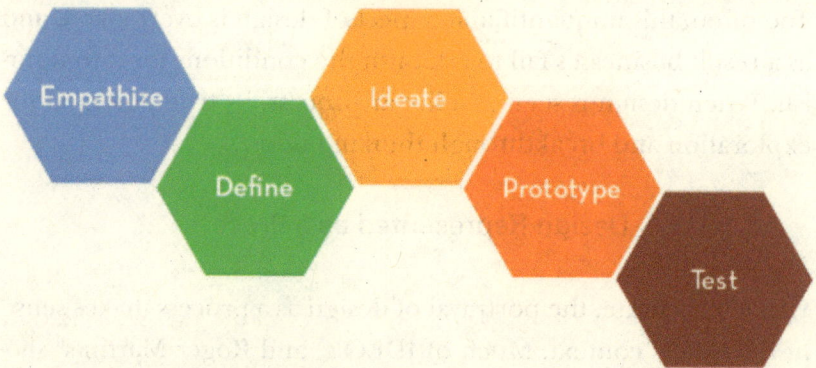

Figure 2.2 *Stanford d.school streamlined design process (Legacy, circa 2012). https://dschool.stanford.edu*

as practicing it. Jon Kolko, formerly principal designer and associate creative director at frog design, and founder of the Austin Center for Design, argues that the intuition designers use to spot patterns comes from years of practicing design on a wide variety of problems. "What many refer to as intuition," he argues, "is not the untaught or unteachable, but instead is a learned understanding and respect of process, molded by experience and refined over a great deal of time and practice."[8]

But the selling of design as a skill anyone could pick up, without years of training, meant that the messy part – the craft of design – was sidelined.

Design as Exploration

While the design *process* has value, it is not the same thing as design. Practice is much less predictable, and designers work in a context where prediction just isn't possible.

Designers work on complex challenges, with no starting place or ending place, that are part of a system, in which acting on one part impacts another part of the system; and in which you can only start to understand the problem by trying to solve it. They are novel problems – not necessarily new to the world, but where the organization is trying to tackle an existing problem in a way that makes sense for its own specific context at a specific time – so replicating past efforts won't work. They are about human experience: understanding and improving the experience of people who are different from you, have different beliefs, experiences, and values – and there are often multiple stakeholders whose priorities may be at odds with one another.

To engage meaningfully with such problems, designers need to question their foundations; to explore their nature, scope, and boundaries; and to see them from unusual perspectives. This demands a unique workstyle, one that emphasizes agility, learning, discovery, and dwelling in the ambiguous problem space.

For managers and other professionals, this exploratory approach can challenge, and seem to undermine, the things they believe to be true and good in work. When designers talk about stepping back and exploring the problem, alarm bells go off for managers who are more accustomed to workstyles that emphasize and value predictability, reliability, and control.

Epistemic Action

Design activities originated in a studio environment, where practitioners drew, modeled, and made physical products and artifacts. As design activities moved to higher orders (see the discussion of Richard Buchanan's "Orders of Design" in chapter 1), design was increasingly aligned with strategy and planning, and less with the original craft. As more managers adopted design thinking as a practice, there has been further distancing between design as a *way of thinking*, and design as a *physical act*.

Drawing and making are forms of active inquiry, allowing individuals to explore and experiment with different perspectives. For example, drawing can be used to sketch out unique design concepts, or to map out complex systems or relationships. This is known as *epistemic action*: actions or practices that help acquire, create, communicate, or verify knowledge or understanding.[9]

The assimilation of design into business and government planning has come with a cost: the loss, or devaluing, of epistemic action. To be understood, designers adapt their methods to match those prevailing in a corporate environment: spreadsheets, PowerPoints, and Gantt charts, rather than sketches and prototypes. Yet the act of drawing and making is not just about producing a physical artefact – it is a way of thinking too. Suppress drawing, and you suppress thinking.

Breakthrough Thinking

Designers have learned to harness design processes to gather the right data, and to ensure they are focusing on the right problem to solve, but process is not enough. To get to a great insight or a great idea – otherwise known as breakthrough thinking – cognitive leaps are required, and for these to happen, the right conditions need to be in place.

Cognitive leaps are significant advancements or breakthroughs in a person's thinking, understanding, or problem-solving abilities. They are sudden shifts in perception or perspective leading to a new level of insight or understanding. Often they are accompanied by a sense of clarity and understanding that seemingly comes out of nowhere.

Cognitive leaps occur when a person has been grappling with a problem or idea for a while, and suddenly a solution or a new perspective presents itself. They involve making connections between different areas of knowledge and integrating them into a new understanding or perspective.

Great insights and ideas need conditions that facilitate cognitive leaps and inspiration. However, design in corporate environments tends to focus entirely on process and not on creating the conditions for breakthrough thinking.

Reflection, and the ability to make connections, are essential. Having time to step away and revisit a problem; getting out of one's environment, such as going to an art gallery or a movie; being exposed to ideas unrelated to the immediate project; elevating the mood and atmosphere of a workspace; working out loud in multi-modal/multi-sensory ways – all of these contribute to breakthrough thinking. However, it is difficult to draw a straight line between these activities and ostensibly more productive outputs. It is hard to make a business case for time to reflect and connect, much less to go to a movie. Too often, leaders focus on enabling the practice and execution of design process and ignore the other elements of the design workstyle that foster breakthrough thinking.

Loosening the Workstyle Bind

The Workstyle bind results from the oversimplification of design, and from organizations' consequent failure to put in place the conditions that foster good design. The designers we interviewed try to loosen this bind by demonstrating what design really means, by making it feel familiar, by being explicit about the different workstyle and mindset, and by applying design to solve the pain points of participants in the process.

Shifting Mentality by Doing

It is difficult to shift mentalities around ways of working by talking about design. Designers have a common mantra, "show, don't tell." People who have been through their first design project often respond with, "Oh, I get it now! You explained it to me, and I thought I had an intellectual grasp of it – but it didn't make sense until I'd been through the process."

Before Chris Conley founded the design firm Gravity Tank, he worked for Motorola. Conley built a reputation as an insightful problem solver and innovator by helping colleagues draw large diagrams that made sense of problems and visualized concepts. Initially, there were no whiteboards or supplies available to facilitate these visual sensemaking and drawing sessions, and he had not built a sufficient reputation to ask for a budget for supplies. He went to a local office supplies store and, out of his own pocket, bought a large roll of paper, masking tape and chart markers so that, rather than just talk about visual work, he could *demonstrate* its value. By focusing on action, Conley facilitated an experience that showed the value of a different workstyle; his approach stuck, and executives became more attuned to design as a result.

Instead of investing too much effort in explaining the rationale, focus on shifting mentality by doing. Sometimes this means being entrepreneurial and venturesome, like Conley, in finding ways to get people to engage in design activities.

Be Explicit about Different Workstyle and Mindset

Formal meetings, boardroom tables, and presentations are the water organizations swim in. Leaders and managers are often oblivious to the ways their default workstyle and attitudes conflict with those designers need. One important approach is to make colleagues aware of the difference in workstyles, and to recognize how each plays a different and key role in the success of the organization.

Figure 2.3 *Foamcore boards, a cheap way to set up wall space.*

Chris McCarthy identified one most important tasks of a design leader as ensuring that leaders come to design meetings with the right mindset. In working with senior leaders at Kaiser Permanente, he developed heuristics around four mindsets that each play an important role in different parts of a project:

- *Strategic mindset:* future sensing, choosing opportunity, whether the problem/opportunity will be relevant in 3 years
- *Explorative mindset:* open, curious, going broader than the team is accustomed to going
- *Generative mindset:* encouraging many ideas, testing, building, trying many more things
- *Implementation mindset:* efficient decision making and operations

To help encourage the leaders to accept the mindset needed for a specific task, McCarthy would get leaders to close their eyes, sit quietly, and meditate at monthly meetings. Each meditation focused on a different mindset, but they followed a pattern: Ground the leaders and thank them for their operational mindset; provide permission to adopt an explorative mindset (leaders need permission to change and become exploratory); at the end close out and let them return to an operational mindset.

One of the benefits of the mindset meditation, he told us, is that everyone adopted the same mindset. In case you are thinking that this is just hippy designer nonsense, all the VPs with whom he worked swore by it, and acknowledged that, unless they were mindful, their operational mindset would leak back into their work.

We asked Chris how he did it. "The first meditation felt kooky; the second meditation became more normal." He persisted, and the leaders adopted it. Half knew Chris and trusted him; and, because the project was focused on mental health and the value of mindfulness, the other half were not resistant to the idea of meditation.

Meditation was a brilliant idea in this situation, but may not work in all environments or for all projects. However, the key to success here is to point out the need for a different mindset, and find a point that *connects* with the audience, while still pushing them beyond their comfort zone. For software designers, for example, try using UX tools to question the brief; to connect with manufacturing engineers, try showing the limitations of project management tools.

Use Design to Solve *Their* Pain Points

For managers, one of the annoying things about designers is that they can be sanctimonious and try to make converts out of stakeholders. Managers do not usually create double binds because of a disagreement with the beliefs and practices of design. Rather, they are singularly focused on achieving their business objective, and are ignorant about, or agnostic to, the methodological path to getting there.

At Toronto's University Health Network, Jen Recknagel uses design to understand the challenges and needs of older adults as they try to support aging in place within the community. Recknagel believes that stakeholders don't care about design or other methods, just about their own objectives.

NORC's stakeholders are more than happy to accept design, she says, when they see it as a vehicle to advance their goals. Similarly, Chris Conley had little pushback from colleagues when he brought in rolls of chart paper and markers because they saw that drawing helped them make sense of their complex problems. The lesson from both was quite plain: Instead of focusing on design itself, focus on helping stakeholders solve *their* problem through design.

If designers, in partnership with organizations, are to redesign value, they need the right conditions to be in place. Due largely

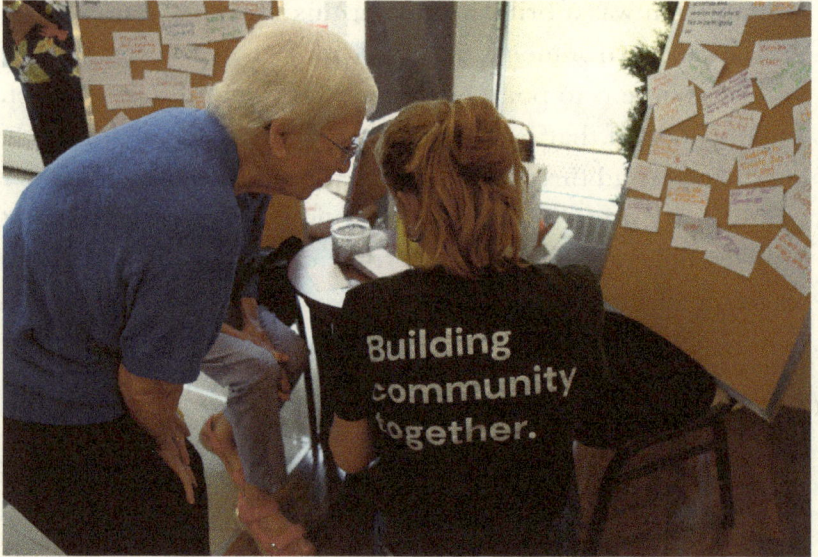

Figure 2.4 *OpenLab workshop with older adult. (Recknagel, OpenLab)*

to ignorance and misunderstanding of design – the result of its overselling to the business community – these conditions are often lacking. The result, as we saw in the opening story to this chapter, is that design falls short, leading to uninteresting ideas, and the self-fulfilling prophecy that "design doesn't work." Clarity, persistence, and courage are needed when dealing with the Workstyle bind.

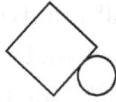

3 The Risk Bind

Organizations tend to be risk-averse, even when they know they have to change. Because design is all about change, designers are more comfortable with uncertainty, and more inclined to embrace risk. Yet while designers need to remain true to their mission of delivering value for users, society and the planet, they also need to be careful to avoid coming off as arrogant and cavalier.

Under CEO Rick Wagoner, General Motors lost about $82 billion between 2005 and 2009. Yet what he regretted most was quashing the electric car (EV1).

Literally. In the 1990s, GM launched the EV1 to fulfill a California mandate for a zero-emission vehicle. Between 1996 and 1999 GM built about 2,500 EV1s and leased them to consumers in California and Arizona. In 2006, after a great deal of lobbying, the California mandate was removed, and the remaining EV1s were recalled. Aside from a few vehicles donated to museums, the rest were crushed.

What happened in GM's executive suite is lost in a fog of competing narratives. But the elements of the decision are easy enough to see. "Sadly," wrote spokesman Dave Barthmuss in a blog post, "despite the substantial investment of money and the enthusiastic fervor of a relatively small number of EV1 drivers ... the EV1 proved far from a viable commercial success."[1] GM invested over $1 billion developing and marketing the EV1, yet managed to lease only 800 vehicles over a four-year period. With such a low volume, GM felt it could no longer supply parts or guarantee the safety of the cars over time. More cynically, perhaps, management may have feared a backlash from GM dealers, since electric cars need no servicing and few repairs.

The choices would have been to double down on a losing proposition, or pull the plug. At the head of an unprofitable company, Wagoner, a former CFO, would have been acutely aware of the risks of continuing with the EV1. But he missed the bigger picture: the massive problem of climate change – already on the radar by the 1990s – and the opportunity for GM to take the lead in sustainable innovation. In 2006, GM's reputation was trashed in Chris Paine's documentary *Who Killed the Electric Car?*[2]

A couple of years later, a fledgling upstart launched its first electric car. That upstart was Tesla.

The world's top automakers are now planning to invest $1.2 trillion by 2030 in EV technology.[3] GM will invest $35 billion by the end of 2025, dwarfing the $1 billion it spent on the EV1. Yet GM continues to hedge its bets: In the short term, it is investing heavily in its traditional V-8 technology, with EVs taking a back seat.[4] Meanwhile, Tesla's investment of $500 billion dwarfs that of GM and other automakers.

It's hard to fault GM's logic: Given what was known at the time, continuing with the EV1 seemed to represent an unnecessary risk. But it's the *un*known – or, as strategic planners say, unknown unknowns – that holds the greatest risk. For this, designers and managers need to think more broadly, beyond what is currently known, while limiting exposure to risk. Often, they fall short.

The Risk Bind

The risk bind happens when organizations need to take measured risks, but are unable, or unwilling, to do so. Knowing the stakes, many organizations hire designers to provide a different perspective, but balk when their ideas stray too far from the tried and true.

Experiencing the Risk Bind

The Risk bind is pervasive in large organizations. Designers experience it in several ways: a focus on avoiding uncertainty; a culture that cannot learn from failure; a bias for incremental, rather than disruptive, change; and denial that risks even exist.

Avoiding Uncertainty

Large organizations crave certainty and predictability, and this conflicts with designers' way of doing things. Patrick Whitney is a leading thinker in the application of design in business and social contexts. Dean emeritus of the IIT Institute of Design, he is Distinguished Research Fellow at Brown University School of Public Health, and wrote the foreword for this book. "Most executives would like to make more of the same thing that they're already making," he told us. "Designers like doing something new ... and if they see that risk is an inherent part of doing something different, then they probably think risk is good."

Uncertainty is inherent in design. In the early stages of a project, design teams often do not know which direction they're going in, and are unable to provide the kind of certainty managers usually demand. "The mindset of engineers and business people is, 'know where you're going before you start going'; [but] designers start going, as a way of figuring out where we should be," said Whitney.

UNKNOWN
PROBLEMS

↑

KNOWN ← → UNKNOWN
SOLUTIONS SOLUTIONS

↓

KNOWN
PROBLEMS

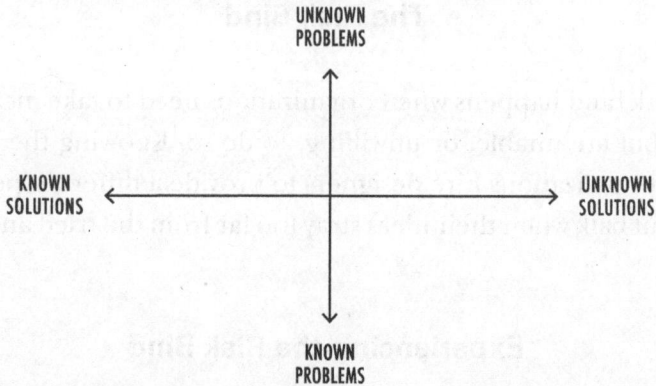

Figure 3.1 *Certainty and uncertainty in problem solving.*
(Sarah Cantor Aye)

Though most managers try to avoid uncertainty, it is the very thing that gets designers excited. We met Sara Cantor Aye of Greater Good Studio, a design studio dedicated to the social sector, in chapter 2. According to Aye, problems can be classified according to the certainty or uncertainty of the problem itself and solutions to it, so you have four quadrants: known problems with known solutions; known problems with unknown solutions; unknown (i.e., ambiguous) problems with known (i.e., previously tried) solutions; and unknown problems with unknown solutions (see Figure 3.1).

Designers are not needed where both the problem and the solution are known – the bottom left quadrant in Figure 3.1. "If the client is like, 'We're sure the problem is this, and we're sure the solution is that' ..." – such as a routine website redesign – "we don't get up in the morning for those kinds of projects," she said with a smile. Nor are they particularly interested in imposing familiar solutions where the problem has not been fully explored: This is the area of false optimism.

Designers can see possibilities where the problem is well understood but needs fresh solutions. But where the problem is tricky, ambiguous, and needs reframing – where neither the problem nor the solution is known – *that's* where designers shine: They seek out the uncertain, the risky, the uncomfortable. It also happens to be the territory that causes managers the most discomfort.

Abhorrence of Failure

Learning from small-scale failure is also inherent to design, yet, in some organizations, the worst thing you can do is to be seen to fail. Dr. Howie Abrams is director of the University Health Network's OpenLab in Toronto. Abrams has succeeded in many disciplines: His eclectic background encompasses anthropology, ethno-musicology, engineering, and a specialty in internal medicine. He once lived with a nomadic tribe in northern Kenya doing ecological research, and helped develop community-based services and research capacity in Northern Ontario, Africa, and Asia.

Abrams understands the need to learn from one's mistakes. However, he said, "In healthcare, you're not allowed to fail." Most of us would be uncomfortable with our doctor being too relaxed about failure, but this isn't what Abrams was talking about: Patient care is one thing, institutional management another. With patient care, it's understood that you need to proceed cautiously and do everything possible to avoid failure – the mantra, after all, is "first do no harm."

But healthcare institutions do much more than look after patients. OpenLab's projects, for example, include a vertical urban farm that provides patient therapy, community engagement, food literacy education, health research, and revenue generation, and that promotes local food; an overdose response network that allows people who use drugs to tap into their social network of people close by who have naloxone; and that uses virtual reality technology to test the impact of simulated environments on patients' health. None of these projects would have been possible without failed experiments along the way.

Many healthcare organizations are allergic to anything that sniffs of failure. Abrams told us of a former boss at UHN who was fond of saying, "I'm always looking for whose neck to wring; who's the person who's going to take the final responsibility for failure?" Abhorrence of failure may be appropriate in patient care, but abhorrence can become pervasive, and *in*appropriate, across an organization's culture. "You can't have that 'blame' philosophy if you're going to try to design or innovate something new," said Abrams. Where there is blame, people will be risk-averse, and innovation will be stifled.

A Bias for the Incremental

Understandably, organizations often prefer to dip a toe in the water. But sometimes, like GM and the electric car, the biggest risk is not being bold enough. Maxims like "let's not boil the ocean" assume that innovation has to proceed in tiny steps. In a science-based culture like healthcare, progress is incremental: what Thomas Kuhn called "normal science," not once-in-a-generation paradigm shifts.[5]

Designers can run into resistance when they look to change things more fundamentally. Rather than talk about boiling oceans, Abrams tries to get people to think differently about problems. Some years ago, before the COVID-19 pandemic, he tried to get UHN interested in virtual care; nobody wanted to know. "I was always told, well, we don't have a strategy." Then, in 2020, with COVID, events took over; suddenly, everyone wanted virtual care. UHN, like most of healthcare, was lurching from crisis to crisis: Before the pandemic, the lack of virtual healthcare was a slow-moving problem, but it didn't seem to constitute a big risk. In 2020, incremental change was suddenly no longer enough: Virtual care *had* to be solved, right away. A more courageous approach could have had a tried-and-tested virtual care system in place when the pandemic hit.

Risk Denial

Sometimes, the riskiest thing you can do is put your head in the sand. Denial of the extent of risk in the status quo – or even that it exists – can also hamper designers.

It can take a great deal of courage for organizations even to acknowledge a problem because it may reflect badly on powerful individuals or destabilize existing power structures. "A big problem is leadership not wanting to acknowledge the problems that they have, in order to create change," said Mount Sinai's Bruno Silva. On one occasion, he was warned by a colleague that the way he was framing an internal problem might undermine company leadership: "They see our problem framing as negative criticism to the work that they're doing, so that their leadership is poor because of all these problems." Designers' perspective could not be more different: For a designer, the word "problem" has a *positive* connotation, because every problem is an opportunity to design something better.

Understanding the Risk Bind

The Risk bind is not just about actual risk; it arises from national and organizational culture. However, designers often exacerbate the problem.

Risk-Averse Cultures

The Risk bind is related to organizational culture, and designers experience it in organizations large and small.

In the best-known approach to culture, the Hofstede cultural framework, national cultures differ on "uncertainty avoidance," the degree to which members of a society feel uncomfortable with uncertainty and ambiguity. The issue is whether a society tries to control the future or just let it happen. With a low score of 35 out of 100 on uncertainty avoidance, for example, the UK is relatively comfortable with risk – certainly compared with Japan, which scores 92.

Within national cultures, organizational cultures differ too, in the degree of control they demand. In a very strict work culture, predictability is valued, internal structure is rigid, and control and discipline are emphasized, while there is little improvisation or surprise; people are very cost-conscious, punctual, and serious.[6]

In one study, German researchers Malte Brettel, Christoph Chomik, and Tessa Christina Flatten developed a model of four cultural types based on their orientation towards stability, order, and control, versus flexibility and change; an *internal* focus on people within the organization versus an *external* focus on its relationship to its environment. From this, they defined four cultural types: Hierarchical, Rational (all about competitiveness and market superiority), Group (about belonging and loyalty), and Developmental (about creativity and external orientation) (see Figure 3.2).

In a survey of German SMEs, they tested how each culture type was related to risk-taking.[7] Not surprisingly, they found that hierarchical cultures, those that preferred high levels of control, mitigated against it. But there were interesting forces at work in the other cultures too. Though hierarchical and group cultures were very different, they were both internally focused, and this meant that group cultures also tended to avoid risk – in all likelihood because of groupthink. Nevertheless, group cultures were less risk-averse than hierarchical cultures, because they had more trust, collaboration, and flexibility.

Externally focused cultures were more comfortable with risk. In rational cultures, which were all about competitive advantage,

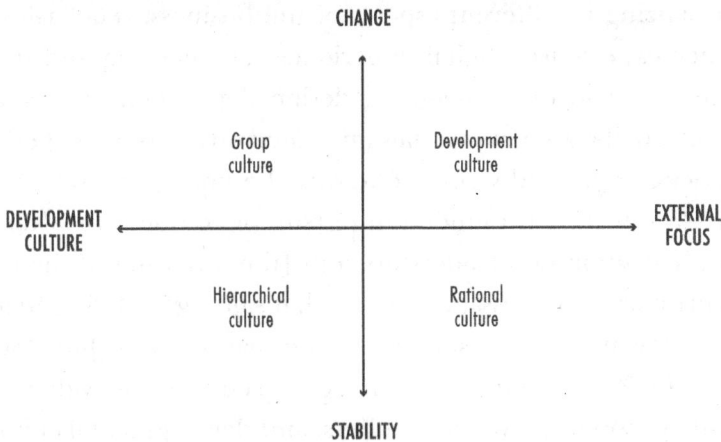

Figure 3.2 *Cultural types. (From Brettel et al.)*

a focus on stability and clear goals encouraged risk-taking. As you might expect, risk-taking was also encouraged in developmental cultures, where the focus was on creativity and external orientation.

At first sight, this looks like good news for designers. Three of the four cultural types encourage *some* degree of risk-taking and innovativeness, albeit for different reasons. So unless you live in a hierarchical culture, you should be able to ask those provocative questions without fear. Right?

Not exactly. Though you may find pockets of different cultures in an organization, the dominant culture is usually hierarchical. Within individual departments, you can find examples of group culture, rational culture, and developmental culture, where employees are creative and externally focused (this might be the culture within the design lab). The cautious approach of the hierarchical culture, however, tends to dominate even where other subcultures exist.

This nuanced picture was evident at TELUS, a large Canadian telco, where aspects of all four culture types were on display. The company was organized on hierarchical lines, with departments specializing in different aspects of the business: retail sales, customer experience, digital experience, engineering and maintenance, and so on. A fledgling design department consisting of about a half-dozen individuals innovated on customer experience, service design, and so on. Following the norms of a rational cul-ture, the team was founded in pursuit of competitive advantage: "We had some new leadership, and [the founding of the design team] became a message around what's going to differentiate us, and allow us to really succeed in the market," said Judy Mellett, the team leader. Within the team, group culture was evident in the mutual support between members, and developmental culture in their open, highly collaborative work style.

Even though the team had its own internal culture, the dominant culture in the company, the one that called the shots, was hierarchical. Risk was tightly controlled, through the threat that the team might be disbanded at any time: "My VP, he says, 'I'll give you a year,'" said Mellett. Naturally enough, given a tight timeframe, the group gravitated to low-risk projects. It made little sense, then or later, for the team to risk *its own* survival in a competitive internal landscape, so significant disruption of the order of things, or of the company's strategy – even when circumstances demanded it – were never in the cards.

How Designers Help Tie the Knots

Designers, however, also contribute to the risk bind. We heard plenty of stories where designers saw themselves as visionaries ahead of their time, innocent victims of systems built to minimize risk and crush innovation in the process. It's true that hierar-chies, in particular, tend to be cautious, and in such environments designers can come across as wild adventurers – "crazy cowboys," as one interviewee put it.

David McGaw, of Google, where he is UX innovation and strategy lead, questions designers' self-image as natural visionaries. For McGaw, *every* strategist – designer or not – needs to be a visionary, but it doesn't come naturally. He calls it *conditioned optimism*, the ability to think freely about possible futures. However, he believes it comes from training and practice, and is not the exclusive domain of designers.

Yet optimism, especially when it glosses over legitimate risk, can tip into arrogance. Junior designers, in our experience, can fixate on a solution and have trouble letting it go. It comes across as if designers feel they alone have the answer, just because they're designers. Their strength at reimagining the world as it could be can easily become the weakness of not being able to compromise or let something go. Naturally, their management colleagues tend to push back.

While recognizing that their job is to look boldly into the future, designers need to show humility. "It's not [that] you're inherently more visionary," said McGaw, "It's just that you're working at it."

Design is a political process in organizations, yet designers are notoriously bad at organizational politics. They tend to assume that support from the top means that everyone else will fall in line, but modern organizations, even hierarchical organizations, do not work that way. They are made up of people, and people have trouble with change, especially if it may endanger their livelihood or make their lives more difficult. Winning an organization over to design isn't just a question of delivering great ideas: It's a process that happens over time, not overnight.

For good reason, many, if not most, internal design programs are run by non-designers: Procter & Gamble's inaugural design program in the early 2000s was run by Claudia Kotchka, a former accountant, while, at RBC Royal Bank, innovation leader Peter Chow's training and background are in risk management. Leaders such as these know how to develop relationships over time across the company. They put people first and take the long view.

Loosening the Risk Bind

In spite of their differences, managers and designers share a great deal of common ground when it comes to risk. At RBC, Peter Chow argues that designers and risk managers are more similar than different. Both look to the future: in the case of designers, to create better outcomes, and, in the case of risk managers, to avoid the worst outcomes. Analyzing the data behind an RBC report on employment,[8] Chow found that designers and risk managers shared 19 of 20 skills. "[In both] you need empathy, you need to understand the situation, you need analytics, you need to be able to really understand a situation and all the contextual gray areas that go into it," he said.

Across the organizations we spoke to, managers and designers have found several ways of loosening the risk bind and bridging their differences. These include making things tangible, making risk explicit, modeling change from the top, and taking a risk yourself.

Make Things Tangible

Rather than wallow in ambiguity, designers can make both the problem and their ideas concrete and, therefore, more approachable.

Bruno Silva made his learning platform tangible by showing a prototype website to senior management. To develop an internal learning platform, Silva needed to create a network and a curriculum, but to begin with, the team did not know which direction the project would take. Yet whenever they talked about the research process, it didn't sit well with leaders who were uncomfortable with the unknown.

Silva found that the way to navigate this was to make the problem, or the solution, tangible. Accordingly, he decided to pivot: Website resources were already part of the plan, so he decided to focus communication with executives on these.

"So they started saying, '*Oh*, it's a website!'" he said. Realizing that executives needed some basis for understanding the plan, Silva replied, "Sure, it's a website," and developed a prototype. By providing a tangible example of what the program might look like, he was able to reduce the uncertainty and perceived risk. From that point onwards, Silva and his team were able to develop the network and the curriculum with full support.

"Even showing evidence quickly on the project," said a designer, "whether it's doing preliminary interviews just to get soundbites, to let them see there is a problem here, or there is excitement around this idea. [Or] you can prototype something really quickly, just to get some proof to then share back, which helps ease the fear."

Going further, some designers position their work as a way to *de-risk* projects. Emmanuel Fragnière is a professor of service design at the University of Applied Science Western Switzerland. Fragnière started his career as a risk analyst and was drawn to design because of its remarkable ability to build and test ideas *in situ* with users and front-line staff. "I realized that the best way to reduce risk was to "tangibilize" ideas in the real world," he said.

By repositioning design as a method that doesn't add risk, but decreases it, designers can leverage their creative problem-solving skills to reduce their colleagues' anxiety.

Model Change from the Top

Senior leaders can play an important part in untying the Risk bind. Drug giant Pfizer's "Dare to Try" program was piloted by Wendy Mayer, design pioneer and Pfizer's vice president, worldwide innovation, and CEO Ian Read. Read wanted to expand the program to encourage employees to take risks and come up with new ideas. But scaling up an initiative like this was not easy: People don't feel empowered to take risks just because the CEO says so.

Then serendipity intervened. In 2014, Pfizer attempted a merger with AstraZeneca. Although the attempt wasn't successful, it brought out the best in Read.

"The CEO actually sent out a note company-wide ... to say that AstraZeneca was his Dare to Try," said Mayer. Read's admission signaled to employees that failure was acceptable, and that they would not be penalized for taking a risk. "That was huge," she added. "[Though] he wasn't successful, it was still important that he tried – and that he tried to bring in new thinking."

Use Your Empathy

Too often, the same designers who advocate empathy towards users fail to show empathy towards their colleagues, who face real risks to their reputation and career – everything from looking ridiculous to termination.

The mandate of managers is to make choices, not wonder about possibilities. Said a design leader at a national health insurance provider, "If you're in a room with non-designers who are making decisions, they don't want you adding more options. They want *less* options ... they think that creativity has its place, but it's not in the C-suite."

Though the comment was intended as bitter criticism, it is a fair reflection of reality: CEOs are paid to make decisions, not to speculate. When designers propose new ideas, the risks for managers are real, and they increase as these ideas get further from what the organization is currently doing. In untying the Risk bind, designers trivialize these risks at their peril.

Designers need to empathize with those who seek certainty. Ariana Shadlyn is a design leader at Canadian insurance provider Manulife. Trained as a designer, working with uncertainty comes naturally to Shadlyn, but she recognizes that leaders who are investing time and money deserve answers, not abstraction: "'What's it going to look like?' [they ask]. 'What exactly is it going to do? Let's go back to our business objectives: How can you guarantee you'll meet them?'"

Internal stakeholders have a legitimate voice: Most of the problems designers deal with have multiple stakeholders, and the design task is to understand how their diverse interests can be reconciled, or built upon, to arrive at the best possible solution.

If designers took empathy seriously, they would develop methods to deal with it. What if, for example, there was a "disciplina" – like a persona – for colleagues inside the organization, to help designers appreciate their goals and the pressures they face? Or an empathy map?[9] Or what about reaching out to the *most* risk-averse stakeholders, listening to them and taking their views into account?

Take a Risk Yourself

But what if nothing works? What if all the concreteness, role modeling, and empathy you come up with don't move the needle? Perhaps then it's time to take a risk of your own.

At UHN, during the COVID-19 pandemic, Abrams was developing a "Friendly Neighbour Hotline," a volunteer-driven program to support low-income seniors with food access. The project needed a floating pool of money to reimburse volunteers for out-of-pocket costs for food and other expenses. Abrams created an account at his own bank and deposited $5,000 of his own money. Once the program was up and running, he approached the hospital for reimbursement. He had no receipts, and the expenditure was outside his mandate – "they went bananas," he said – but he did it because it was necessary to move the project forward. After a struggle, and a warning that this was a one-time thing, he was reimbursed.

If Abrams's approach seems extreme, remember that some of medicine's greatest discoveries have been made by physicians who took great personal risks.[10] In 1769, William Stark conducted an experiment in diet and nutrition by going for 31 days on nothing but bread, water, and a little sugar. Then he gradually introduced other foods, one at a time. However, he failed to include citrus fruits or vegetables. In less than a year, he died of scurvy at the age of twenty-nine – but his research led to the realization that vitamin C deficiency was implicated in scurvy. Similarly, Dr. Barry Marshall drank bacteria from a sick patient in a "brew." He became severely ill, but confirmed his hypothesis that ulcers were caused by *H. pylori* bacteria and could be cured by antibiotics. In 2005, Marshall won the Nobel prize in physiology for his discovery.

Not everyone is willing or able to put $5,000 of their own money – or their life – on the line. Abrams clearly understood the risk that he might not be reimbursed – but he felt it was worth the personal risk. Concreteness, courage, and willingness to do what's necessary go a long way in motivating those around you.

The Biggest Risk?

Both managers and designers would benefit from a broader perspective on risk. Managers need to get away from their bias for the short-term bottom line, and designers for the user, to think more broadly. Like the GM management team, there are plenty of both who fail to look at the bigger implications of what they are doing: climate change, inequality, exploitation, and the many ills that plague our planet, as direct or indirect results of short-term innovation with only the user or the organization in mind.

As Whitney put it, "In many ways, human-centered design is really about selling more stuff in a world that already has too much stuff." Are designers and managers both missing the biggest risk of all?

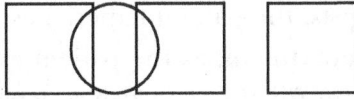

4 The Silo Bind

Silos, and silo mentality, are the enemy of design. Because designers think in broad terms about users and context, they need to work across silos and have unrestricted access to users. Yet silos are a necessary part of organizational life. Designers need to navigate around, and even transcend, organizational silos, while avoiding creating their own "design silo."

Human needs do not map onto corporate structures. Some years ago, while kicking off a workshop for Mt. Sinai Hospital in Toronto, we saw this in stark relief.

In a brightly lit room at the University of Toronto's Rotman School of Management, about 40 physicians, nurses, and administrators were assembled in teams. In preparation for the session, each participant was asked to submit a story about patient experience. Based on the stories, it was clear that participants had a high degree of empathy for patients.

Thinking he might start the day with an easy question, the session leader asked the group where the patient experience began and where it ended. At first there was confused silence, then a low murmur as participants exchanged quizzical looks – surely, they seemed to be saying, the answer was obvious.

For the radiologists, the patient experience began at the door of the radiology department, as the patient entered, and ended when they left. Ditto for the emergency department. For every department in the hospital, the answer was the same: The patient experience began with their entry into the department and ended with their exit.

Hospitals are highly structured organizations, where individual departments focus tightly on their own specialization. When a patient passes from one department to the next, there is a handover, in the form of a file that is updated as more information becomes available. The patient moves through a series of separate, distinct experiences.

Seen from the patient's point of view, however, the experience is a single thing: It begins when they first encounter symptoms, continues through visits to various parts of the medical system – family doctor, emergency department, back and forth to various specialists, imaging, surgery, rehabilitation, and so on – and ends in some resolution, hopefully for the better. When you look at the *entire* experience, you can see the places where things often go wrong: incomplete information, poor handovers between departments, redundant tests, and the frustration reported by many patients at being asked for the same information over and over.

There was a palpable shift in the mood as this new perspective sank in. Merely to understand the patient experience, let alone improve it, you had to let go of silos and think holistically.

Later in the day, teams were asked to select a project to improve patient experience. Many chose projects that straddled the boundaries between departments. One decided to develop a concierge system, a hub to orient patients through their hospital experience;

another developed a patient dashboard, to improve the quality of handovers from emergency to radiology. Yet challenging as it was for participants even to *think* across silos, this was only the beginning. Bringing cross-silo projects like these to fruition takes a great deal of time, effort, and scarce resources.

The Silo Bind

It is widely accepted that organizational silos impede innovation.[1] But they remain persistent, and pernicious, in the day-to-day lives of designers. The Silo bind happens when organizations support the intent of design, but silos, and the silo mentality associated with them, throw obstacles in its path. Too often, designers respond by circling the wagons and building a silo of their own to protect their work.

Experiencing the Silo Bind

Because it is in the nature of design to work across organizational boundaries, the effects of silos are felt keenly by designers. They surface in reluctance to share access to critical stakeholders, information, and methods; in lack of accountability; in lack of collaboration; and in failure to implement projects.

Access to Stakeholders

Silos often create barriers between designers and the research they need to do. To develop insights and test prototypes, designers regularly need access to two groups: subject-matter experts and end users. Yet they are often denied access. Subject-matter experts tend to have little time, or incentive, to talk to designers, and customers are "owned" by the sales team, who may be concerned that designers could pester or annoy customers or say things that conflict with the company's brand message.

In private health insurance, client relationships take shape over time, as clients' lives change. At one insurance company, the department responsible for insurance and investment products (known as "transitional" products) realized that developing a relationship early with the client, and maintaining it over time, would allow it to understand how clients' lives were changing and provide them with the most appropriate products. However, the teams that had access to clients on existing plans, such as group pensions or group health, had no incentive to support or develop these long-term relationships. As a result, the transitional benefits team was stymied in its efforts to understand its clients.

Client access is not the only issue: Silos compete with each other for methodologies too. As one designer told us, "I tried to do a workshop to do the service blueprint, and then the process engineer went to complain that I was stepping on her toes: I shouldn't be doing a service blueprint, because it's something that they actually do as engineers."

Even starting up a design lab can create friction. When TELUS set up its design team, they tried to decide on a name. "What do we call this?" asked Judy Mellett, then newly appointed as director. "If we said 'customer experience management,' there was another team that sees themselves as owning customer service: They were going to get their nose out of joint if we said, 'We're the customer experience team.' If we said, 'We're the user experience team,' now the digital team was going to say, 'That's ours …'" The team settled on service design, but not before it had become clear that, to get itself off the ground, it would have to navigate around established and powerful teams.

Eventually, design teams usually find a way of dealing with issues like these. But, by using up time and energy on internal debates, they derail the team from its main mandate of solving problems for users and stakeholders.

Lack of Accountability

No innovation is useful unless it is implemented. In theory, silos *should* make it clear who is responsible for what, but in practice they often blur accountability and derail implementation.

Marlies van Dijk founded and led the Alberta Health Services Design Lab, an initiative to "kickstart discussions that help us make meaning, breathe life into structures with human-centred design and develop collaborative governance." AHS Design Lab's work includes innovative food service to clients of Carewest, one of the largest care providers in Canada; developing a vaccination clinic for 2,500 new immigrant meat-plant employees; and supporting youth in drug recovery.

Despite the lab's impressive record, van Dijk's frustration with silos was clear. Within the tight boundaries of hospital silos, any dissension was suppressed. As a result, people had become passive and accepting of an unacceptable status quo.

On one occasion, she asked an emergency nurse what she was thinking when patients came in who would be better treated in other parts of the healthcare system. "Why are they here?" she answered, suggesting they ought to be transferred to other parts of the hospital or to community care. But she corrected herself right away: "I'm not allowed to say that out loud ... we're supposed to take everyone in – that's the code for the Emergency Department, right? You don't question." Even questioning the way things were done was out of bounds.

"Dissension among the frontline is really important," commented van Dijk: "having a culture where people say, 'Why are we doing this? Or, is this *really* what we're doing?'" Lack of accountability meant that patients could be shifted around without anyone accepting responsibility, while command-and-control structures within the silos suppressed any dissent. "In medicine and health care, we're rank and file," she added. "We're like a military model."

Few armies would consider this an effective way to wage a war. "We just circle around," said van Dijk. "No one's really in charge. No one's really holding anyone accountable. We're all great people, but there's very little accountability in our system."

Lack of Collaboration

Because questioning is suppressed, there is no incentive for frontline staff to upset things by collaborating with those they see as outsiders – like designers.

Other departments often see designers as a nuisance, at best. At the Mayo Clinic in Rochester, Minnesota, the Center for Innovation undertook design projects across the entire hospital and its satellite clinics. But they weren't always welcomed. "When you turn up on a Monday morning to do an experiment, the desk staff – they're just not going to want you near them," said Lorna Ross, the Center's former director. "They don't know why you're there; they're not going to really trust you. It's just really disruptive to them; there's not a lot of value to them; there's no incentives."

However, designers can undermine their own projects too. At Kaiser Permanente, an innovation consultancy was tasked with a way of improving administration of medications by nurses. Any interruptions at the critical moment when the nurse is calculating the dose can lead to mis-dosing, with potentially fatal results. Yet in a fast-moving environment, it is difficult to find uninterrupted time.

The consultancy came up with an elegant solution: a sash nurses would wear when they were measuring medication, as a visual signal to others that they needed to focus on what they were doing. The idea gained a great deal of support and recognition, and has been widely cited as an example of good design in healthcare.

But it had one major flaw: Though nurses were involved in creating the sash, the team responsible for implementing it was not. "We have these little groups," reflected Debbie Cotton, director, leadership development, "in different functions in the organization, like the design consultancy ... who are working on solving problems. And they solve the problem, and then toss it over the fence to the place where it has to get implemented. And that's where it falls apart."

When designers toss ideas over the fence, the motivation to take them forward is lacking; moreover, seemingly irrational obstacles pop up. "Process is like, 'Oh, but this is my area. *You're* not doing that,'" one perplexed designer told us, "and they never did it. So we were like, 'OK, you're telling me that you're not going to do that – but you don't let *me* do it.'"

Understanding the Silo Bind

Silos deservedly get a bad rap among designers and innovators. Though silos are there for a reason, they mitigate against the systems perspective that is essential to good design, they isolate the organization from its customers, and they give rise to what is known as a silo mentality. Designers, too, can create silos of their own.

Why Silos Exist

According to Harvard Professor Harold J. Leavitt, there are good reasons for silos to exist: They provide order and security, clear career paths, and "remain the best available mechanism for doing complex work."[2]

But not *all* complex work. If you are the Catholic Church and you want priests to adhere strictly to Church doctrine, hierarchy is your friend; if you are the military and you want to commandeer soldiers in battle, silos can give you deep specialist expertise. If you think business is like the Church or the military – as undoubtedly some CEOs still do – then you will see silos as the natural organization form. And they *are* useful for repetitive processes, like manufacturing widgets of consistent quality, at minimal cost, in predictable environments.

However, there's an alternative explanation, less flattering to CEOs: By dividing up the less powerful, silos allow the powerful to maintain their position.[3] They accomplish this by suppressing questioning, ensuring compliance, and limiting flexibility.

Yet even organizations like the Church and the military now face challenges that demand a more nimble approach than silos can provide. As the world changes ever more rapidly, as technology advances at breakneck speed, silos seem ever more cumbersome.

Silos, and the hierarchies that create them, are widely criticized – not by designers, but by management scholars too.[4] They are rife with communication problems, abuses of authority, turf wars, risk aversion, and destructive competition. According to activist David Graber and Comparative Archeology Professor David Wengrow, they are rooted in Western culture and exclude other ways of knowing and making decisions.[5]

Design demands a broader, system-wide perspective. Silos hinder this perspective, because they isolate the organization from its customers and give rise to a mentality that prevents sharing; and because designers themselves can get trapped within their own silo mentality.

The Systems Perspective

As we saw earlier, patient experience in healthcare runs across different departments in a hospital. To design a patient experience, or any experience for that matter, you need to appreciate the *context* within which the experience happens – and that context includes the other parts of the system the user has encountered or expects to encounter. Silos are intended to maximize the efficiency of delivering established products and services, but experiences cannot always be divided up.

In many situations, some of the silos lie outside the organization. Some experiences, such as coffee shops, are self-contained: You go in, buy your coffee, and enjoy it either on-site or on your way to work. An airline, however, has only limited influence over customer experience: The passenger may book through Expedia or a similar site, check in with a network partner, endure security checks and airport food, fly with a network partner, and have baggage handlers misplace their bags that end up circling in luggage carousels somewhere in the world. Any failure within this experience can affect the passenger's perception of the airline itself, which may have little to do with the problem.

For good economic reasons, organizations – such as airlines that coordinate routes with network partners, or telcos that outsource maintenance to independent contractors – regularly contract out part of the user experience. (Some arguably do so for more nefarious reasons, such as cheap labor, poor regulation, and absence of unions). When they do so, they relinquish control of the experience and, more importantly, limit their ability to innovate. It's a classic example of robbing tomorrow to feed today: Outsourcing may work for the existing business, but the benefits come at the cost of crimping the choices the organization can make for the future.

Isolating the Organization from Customers

Silos may be a logical organization form for goods, but are less logical for services. As we will see in chapter 5, the model of exchange in economics is a "goods-dominant" one that focuses on transactions. Services, by contrast, focus on relationships.[6]

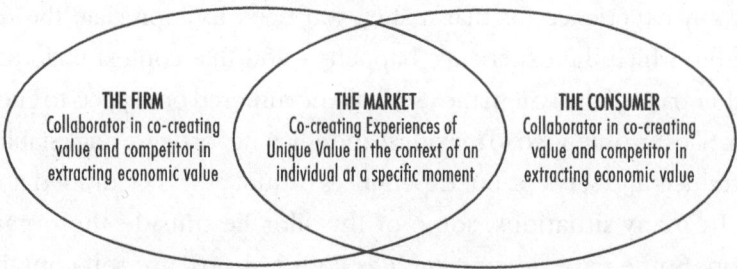

Figure 4.1 *Value co-creation. (Prahalad and Ramaswamy)*

For many businesses, customers exist as assets to be exploited, rather than people to help through their day. Two decades ago, in *The Future of Competition*, the late C.K. Prahalad and Venkat Ramaswamy argued for a new vision of customers.[7] In a 2004 paper, they argued that the traditional conception of value creation positions customers "outside the firm."[8] In models like Michael Porter's value chain, the firm created and delivered value to a customer, who would either accept or reject it, but did not participate in value creation.[9] This model was outdated, they wrote, and the future belonged to companies that *co-created* value with customers.

Even now, Prahalad and Ramaswamy's vision has failed to take hold in many organizations, who only talk to customers at the point of value extraction, not value creation. When a customer "belongs" to the sales team, it means that the customer is a resource to be mined, or a passive automaton, ripe for persuasion to buy something they don't need. This is clear from the common practice among telcos of "upselling" customers who call in for help with a technical or service delivery problem.

Silo Mentality and the Need to Share

Silos have another shortcoming: They have an insidious effect on those who work in them.

Brand management in consumer goods companies often deliberately fosters internal competition. Management trainees are selected for their drive and ambition and pitted against each other to compete for resources. The system is based on the theory that competition between brands brings out the best in everyone, and that any conflicts can be resolved between senior managers, at the top of the brand silos. As an example, one perverse result of this system is that Unilever simultaneously markets Dove, a brand based on supporting women and "real beauty," and Axe, a brand that has promoted a highly sexualized view of women.

Internal competition also risks producing a *silo mentality*. As we have seen, silos may have their uses, but there is not much good to say about a silo mentality. It creates a culture of "us versus them," mistrust, and a propensity to black-and-white thinking, where bad things are blamed on other departments and undeserved credit taken for good things. They create "vertical tunnel vision," held together by hierarchical dominance, that shuts out the wider organizational world, fostering narrow-mindedness and prejudice[10] – a world of Dilberts, trapped in their cubicles.

Silo mentality is tough to get rid of. The origin of the silo metaphor is the tall grain silos scattered across the North American prairies, each separate and distinct from its neighbors. Another side of this metaphor was not lost on Freudian psychologists, some of whom compared the "machines" created by organizations to genitals.[11] Later researchers found the analogy irresistible. "The tall 'silo' would have distinctive phallic properties, which then persecute its inhabitants," argued one paper. "This recognition returns us to ... the deeply embedded dynamics of dominance and submission of the vertical axis of organizational life."[12] Try to chop the silo down, and ... well, you can see where the metaphor takes you.

Whatever your metaphor, silo mentality is oppressive, culturally embedded and difficult to shift. Silos, and silo mentality, are another of design's organizational enemies. In our research, we saw persistent frustration with the barriers thrown up by organizational silos. One interviewee, at a major Canadian bank, told us that the landing page of its website was not developed on the basis of customer needs, but perfectly reflected the company's internal turf wars: The most prominent space was given to the most powerful constituencies within the bank.

Designers' Silo Mentality

Designers themselves, however, are not immune to the siren call of silos. In seeking to protect their work from the pressure to conform to cultural norms, designers can create their own silos and come across as superior and arrogant as a result.

When a Swedish design team was designing automotive accessories for the Chinese market, it developed some initial ideas and decided to consult with other teams in the company, such as engineering. But Evan, the lead designer, had scant regard for these other stakeholders, viewing them as one-dimensional, blind to the possibilities the design team created. "They have zero idea, they don't even know that there's another world," he told his team. "It's like that book, called *Flatland.* It's an amazing book … a journey, where you meet people in different dimensions, so first you encounter one image: It's just one guy, a dot, and he doesn't [know anything about anything]."

Evan was referring to the 1884 book *Flatland: A Romance of Many Dimensions,* a satirical novella by Edwin Abbott Abbott. In the book, a square, living in a two-dimensional world, dreams of a visit to a one-dimensional world of points and lines, which are unable to see the square as anything other than a set of points on a line. Unsuccessfully, the square attempts to convince the points and lines of the existence of a second dimension.

The other stakeholders needed to be "educated," said Evan, in "Flatland education; they need to be taken into this three-dimensional world ... to have that epiphany: 'Wow, maybe there are other areas that we didn't even see.'"

With attitudes like this, it would hardly be surprising if other departments were reluctant to work with the design team, and they could hardly be blamed for dragging their heels when it came to implementing their ideas.

In our experience, designers can be too protective of their ideas in the face of organizational silos. Their superpower is to see the world as it could be – but, too often, not as it is. Designers can become fixated on an ideal state that is not feasible in the current organizational structure, and fail to acknowledge the legitimate needs of their counterparts in other departments.

Loosening the Silo Bind

Even within the most rigid organizational structures, designers have found ways of coping and collaborating across silos and even subverting them to their advantage. Some have found ways to distribute design across organizational silos; to create collaborative cross-silo teams; to manage around user journeys rather than organizational specializations; to combat the silo mentality; and to combat their own silo mentality.

Distribute Design across Silos

Design initiatives within organizations are typically distinct from the rest of the organization and have a high degree of autonomy, usually under the protection of a design enthusiast high up in the hierarchy. But there are exceptions.

The Australian Tax Office was one. In government, few things are quite as certain as the annual round of budget cuts. In the absence of hard deliverables or a readily calculated return on investment, a design lab can easily become a target. To head this off, the ATO embedded its design program within silos across the organization. "We built all these islands of capability through the organization that were stitched together by the brand of 'design,' but they weren't centrally funded," said John Body, one of the program's founders. Instead, design was seeded throughout the ATO's bureaucracy.

Rather than try to fight organizational silos, the ATO chose to live within them. This made the ATO program more resilient: If you wanted to cut design, you would have to cut multiple budgets rather than just one. At the same time, it straddled silos by meeting regularly: conferences and communities of practice brought designers together from across the organization to share issues they faced in common.

It's an attractive idea, but it has a significant downside: Designers can have a tough time standing up to the prevailing culture within the departmental silo they are assigned to. The Mayo Clinic tried something similar. "We had this hope that we could … put service designers in different departments, … and they got destroyed in those environments. We had to pull them out," said Lorna Ross. "I was kind of sad about the fact that the culture's not ready yet for a distributed model, because they're [designers] just too vulnerable," she went on.

This could be mitigated by seeding small groups of designers, rather than individuals, in other departments, and giving them plenty of central support, as the ATO did, through regular conferences and community-of-practice workshops. However, embedding designers in this way naturally restricts their thinking to what benefits their own silo; it inevitably means that the designers will be reluctant to challenge the status quo.

Create a Collaborative Team

Sean Molloy is director, Quality, People-Centred Care and Care Transitions at North York General Hospital. His day-to-day role is leading service design, but his team includes three engineers. This both provides innovation capacity and allows him to be selective about the projects he takes on. Within his team, he is accustomed to bringing design and engineering together to improve patient experience.

Molloy sees too much emphasis on the differences between designers and engineers. "Where I think designers ... have made a mistake is in thinking that they're different from the other change makers in the organization. I think what we need to do is actually bring them all together and say, 'we're *all* motivated by change.'"

His team has succeeded in bringing about significant change across silos, particularly during the COVID pandemic. "It's been remarkable to see a service designer with a Lean engineer, that they're both on the same page," he said. "They're both motivated by 'you know what? We're going to crush the experience here.'"

While he finds that designers and engineers work well together, his team lacks the broader system view needed for disruptive change. "If you're someone that wants to reinvent the healthcare system, don't work in a hospital that is part of the healthcare system. You need to work at a system level," he said.

Pharmaceutical giant Bristol Myers Squibb took the idea of system-level thinking to heart when it decided to improve communication of complex health topics to patients. Traditionally, the industry communicated primarily with physicians and reused the same information in patient communications – much of which was, naturally, incomprehensible to patients.

Previous attempts to be more patient-centered were limited by the experience of people inside the organization and advertising agency partners who were entrenched in the status quo. The answer required bringing in perspectives from outside of their industry.

Led by design studio Bridgeable, BMS embarked on a project, Universal Patient Language (UPL), that aimed to go above and beyond industry standards in communicating complex health topics to patients. From the start, they involved stakeholders from across the healthcare system: 161 healthcare providers, 233 patients, 81 caregivers, and 79 other stakeholders: social workers, pharmacists, advocacy groups, and insurance companies among others. In 29 co-creation sessions, each lasting about eight hours over two days, participants collaborated in activities to build prototypes of new communications.

The combination of external perspectives from across the health system and designers who could translate their knowledge into improved patient communications was profound.

UPL ended up comprising a set of principles, tools, and stewardship. It was a success with patients, who appreciated seeing the information broken down using plain language and visual symbols. It was also adopted by healthcare centers around the world. Importantly for BMS – and for organizations interested in design – it showed the power of co-designing and collaborating with stakeholders across the entire system.

Manage around the User Journey

Silos are built to optimize the organization's need, not the user's need. What if this could be subverted? In chapter 3, we met Dr. Howie Abrams at OpenLab in Toronto's University Health Network. With over 30 years on the front line of clinical care, Abrams is an odd fusion of veteran and rebel. With a bright, mischievous air, he describes himself as anti-authoritarian.

OpenLab grew out of a predecessor lab, the Center for Innovation in Complex Care (CICC). In doing so, it switched from a focus on problems defined by the organization, to prioritizing patients' problems. Realizing that this would create friction with UHN, OpenLab put distance between itself and UHN.

Yet OpenLab takes deliberate steps to bridge its team culture and that of UHN. Between innovators and institutions lies what Abrams calls an "adaptive space," where ideas are further nurtured and developed before being brought into the institution. OpenLab adjusts its structure and behavior as needed: a kind of strategic ambiguity, where OpenLab is a "loosely tethered satellite, which actually changes its relationship, constantly, depending on what the circumstances are."

When large healthcare institutions were stymied by the COVID outbreak, OpenLab's flexible structure allowed it to be nimble in providing urgently needed services to seniors. "Virtually within 10 days, we had a full network up and running to deliver services to seniors," said Abrams. In the Friendly Neighbour Hotline project, a team of 700 volunteers completed small grocery runs across Toronto, and delivered such items as groceries, medication, and household cleaners to seniors' homes.

It's not easy to take an independent path within a tightly controlled hierarchy. But the OpenLab example shows that it *is* possible, with the right combination of professional credibility, independent funding, flexibility – and chutzpah.

Other leaders are going further, suggesting that organizations must realign their operations around services. In the book *The Service Organization*, Kate Tarling recommends repositioning teams around services: "Map the service together. Build roadmaps together. Do user research together. Choose options together. Working with each other can be hard and messy. People are different. But it is still worth it to do it together."[13] Referencing Wright's law (also known as the experience curve, stating that costs fall with increases in scale), Tarling explains that organizations get better at building services and experiences together not because of scale, but because each time people perform a task they do it better. By organizing around specific services, the designerly way of working can become the default model, as organizations focus on delivering better experiences.

Use Stories to Combat the Silo Mentality

While designers are increasingly taking on leadership roles, many leaders of successful design teams leverage in-house networking and storytelling to great effect. At TELUS, Judy Mellett had no design qualifications – she held a B.Com. degree and had a background in retail, marketing, and pricing analysis before becoming an innovation leader – but she was a master storyteller.

During the COVID pandemic, she led a project to mitigate loneliness among long-term care residents in Ontario through apps and communication technology. Like Abrams at UHN, she dodged and wove her way through the corporate hierarchy to create space for a project that was primarily about social impact, rather than the traditional bottom line. "Let's focus on the users first," she told her team, "I'll keep the business at bay for now."

And she did, by telling stories. As she did so, she made full use of emotions. One of the care residents attended a virtual wedding. Apps for games such as bingo and Scrabble brought residents together.

Said Mellett, "One of the residents said, 'This allows me to be part of the world ... when I was put in this home, it felt like a prison. This lets me be part of the greater world at large, and to feel human again.'" Even in a technology-based organization, stories that reflect human impact had great power to instill a sense of common purpose and break down the silo mentality.

Combat Your Own Silo Mentality

As people focus on what they do best and form teams around the skills they have in common, a silo mentality seems a natural way of being. Designers are no exception. Because silos are such a hindrance to good design, designers need to set the tone by disrupting their own silos.

Designers need to be aware that they come with baggage and have limitations of their own. The image of the designer as prima donna is not far beneath the surface, and any hint of arrogance – such as that displayed by Evan in the automotive accessories project – will only bolster it.

Niceness matters. In Copenhagen, the Danish government established MindLab to help public servants develop an "outside-in" perspective that looked at services from the point of view of the user, who did not see the distinction between different silos, and expected an integrated experience.

However, preaching about an integrated experience was not enough. MindLab also needed to engage the ministries by sending people to them who were not merely competent, but also "nice": who showed humility and were pleasant to deal with. Along with a strong understanding of the public sector and a citizen-centered perspective, niceness became one of the lab's primary criteria in recruiting talent.

Language is fundamental too, and one of the easier things to control when it comes to crossing silos. "Design is in my title, but I definitely play down this designer speak," said Mike Lovas, director, Design and Innovation, Cancer Digital Intelligence at Toronto's University Health Network. Lovas is a professional designer, with an academic background in design and biomedical engineering. "I just use the language of whatever setting it is," he told us. "Whether it's with patients or with clinics, or with administrative staff or leadership, I use whatever language is appropriate."

But combating one's own silo mentality is not just about window dressing: True humility is called for. With the rise of strategic design, design schools sometimes give their students the illusion that the strategy courses they take qualify them to contribute to strategic decisions with the executive team. Nothing could be further from the truth. "We were told 'you'll be working on strategy,'" said one designer, a graduate of a large US design school that promotes the strategic view. "That's bullshit. Elon Musk isn't going to ask you what to do."

Designers need to recognize that silos are not mere obstacles between them and the end user, but are users in their own right, with interests and motivations of their own.

The silo metaphor for organizational specialization is perhaps overused, suggesting a greater degree of rigidity than needs to be the case. Silos have clear downsides, but they are not going away any time soon. The biggest silos are those in the mind – and, with the right approach, minds can be changed.

5 The Business Model Bind

A great deal of business and government is founded on a philosophy of value extraction, in the pursuit of short-term profits or efficiency. Many designers in organizations serve the value-extraction model – yet they have the capacity and skills to think bigger: to redesign value to improve lives, promote equality, reduce injustice, and help bring about a more sustainable world.

It's widely accepted that good design is good for business.[1] Yet when one telco wanted to redesign the experience of renegotiating mobile phone plans, design and business didn't seem quite so aligned.

As a national provider of phone and data services, mobile was a core part of the company's business – yet customers consistently ranked the service experience poorly. To address this, the company hired a design consultancy. Early research showed that customers wanted greater transparency and were frustrated – especially if they had been loyal for years – when they heard that other people were getting a better deal.

The consultancy's designers went to work redesigning the experience to increase transparency. However, they ran into immediate resistance from within the organization. From the telco's perspective, transparency wasn't always a good thing: Practices like complex plans that obscured pricing and incentivizing sales reps to maximize customers' spend were considered essential to business success – even if it led to some customers feeling duped.

ARPU, or average revenue per user, is a key metric that affects the share price of publicly traded telcos; the higher the number, the more confidence the market has that an organization can maximize efficiency and profit. Since the organization's stock value was tied to increasing ARPU, fundamental parts of their business model, from the structure of phone plans to the training of call center representatives, were engineered to increase customers' spending.

The design team fully understood the company's need to generate revenue from customers. Yet its perception of value seemed out of touch with its customers, and with broader social movements and regulatory changes to increase transparency and accountability. You only needed to open Reddit to see how enraged customers had pushed federal regulators to change the length of mobile contracts and provide consumers with more options.

Knowing their internal environment, managers who hired and worked directly with the design team were unsurprised at the resistance. Yet these differing perspectives on value indicated a seemingly irreconcilable bind on how to redesign the experience.

The Business Model Bind

Boland and Collopy noted in their classic book *Managing as Designing* that a design attitude is concerned with coming up with good alternatives, whereas a decision attitude, the attitude of most managers, is concerned with choosing between existing alternatives.[2] It is assumed that designers and managers are trying to accomplish the same thing, but our interviewees suggested that this may not always be the case.

For designers, what matters most is understanding people and systems, and creating something of value. Nothing is taken for granted, and everything is seen as designable, including the organization itself. The Business Model bind describes the conflict between designers' expectations to apply design to *create* value for users and society, and a business model that sees design as a way to *extract* value, by increasing revenue and finding efficiencies.

CHRIS'S DESIGN JOURNEY

Chris Ferguson is director of the iSchool Institute at University of Toronto, where he also leads industry-partnership projects. Chris was founder and CEO of the service design firm Bridgeable, where he oversaw an award-winning team serving clients ranging from Fortune 500 companies to not-for-profits. He sold the firm to employees in 2024.

Chris started his career far from the world of both designers and managers. After earning an undergraduate degree in Restoration Ecology, he founded and ran an organic farm on Vancouver Island, inspired by how local First Nations had traditionally cultivated the land. As a board member with the local organic producers association, he fought for the inclusion of more native plants, many of which were threatened by extinction due to postcolonial practices.

Organic farming was meaningful work, but at a certain point, Chris feared for his ability to make ends meet. Ultimately, he decided to go to business school and study entrepreneurship. It was there that he fell in love with design, and came to believe the combination of business and design could be a powerful force for change.

After graduation, Chris founded an industrial design firm that could do corporate work while having space to explore sustainable and social design. An award-winning concept for a sustainable toilet was a notable early success. The firm pitched one project after another and entered competitions with a sustainability focus. Tellingly, almost none of it materialized into paid work.

Over time, the company, now named Bridgeable, shifted to serving corporate clients. Using the emerging methods of service design, Chris and his team promised a human, experiential lens that was missing inside many companies. He began teaching design to professionals within the University of Toronto's MBA, GPLLM, and Masters of UX Design programs.

Bridgeable was successful. The company grew to over 50 designers. Some of the country's largest companies became clients. But while Bridgeable benefited from the growing adoption of design inside corporations, Chris saw how often the design process simultaneously became mechanized and measured in ways that undermined value beyond profit. In practice, companies often chose extracting value over creating it.

Each year, in keeping with its values, Bridgeable conducted a major pro bono project for a different social sector client. One year, the client was a group working on federal policy changes around homelessness. Because homelessness disproportionately affects First Nations, racialized, and LBGTQ+ youth, the project required looking more deeply into the structural forces of inequity. The results challenged how Chris himself had always applied design to creating value inside companies. The old ways of working felt inadequate to deal with these systemic issues. They required broadening the scope of how problems were framed and taking new approaches to design.

Chris refocused yet again, dedicating himself to evolving the practices of both design and management. That sense of purpose is at the heart of both his work on this book and his current approach to applied projects.

Experiencing the Business Model Bind

In the value-extraction model of business, and in the cost-obsessed realm of government, efficiency is king; in that of designers, elegantly solving users' problems takes precedence. In practice, these differences are visible to designers in the false certainty given by numbers – the organizational obsession with measuring everything according to its contribution to the bottom line – in the dehumanization of designers and users, and in distancing the organization from users.

The False Certainty of Numbers

Many design leaders see too much emphasis placed on KPIs (Key Performance Indicators) and spreadsheets that measure the wrong things, and provide fictitious – often, consciously fictitious – numbers.

Sinead Wickham, manager at Bridgeable, told us that introducing financial targets at the wrong point can get in the way of creating value for both organizations and users. Her team was digitizing an outdated service platform, and she praised the client for its genuine wish to learn from people to uncover what they needed.

"But when we're trying to tell the story back to their organization," she said, "the business leads will drop in big graphs from Excel to say, it's a $25 million dollar opportunity – or some amount they've made up. They refer to those as 'wild-ass guesses' … so they can get buy-in from other people at the organization." Inserting made-up numbers into the process had real repercussions for the design process, at a stage when the team was exploring possibilities: "Now we're trying to backfill, to match up our research goals with those numbers," she said.

As an experienced design consultant, Wickham was accustomed to delivering economic value to organizations. "I do get the need to show business value and talk about numbers," she said. But she was critical of what she called "a lot of needing to know." Designers could live with not knowing until they learned from users what they *should* be measuring to show the value to the business; but because the ultimate goal was value extraction, managers had to know right away how much value was there to be extracted. So they forced a number onto the design – no matter that the number was imaginary.

Even if the numbers are real, they may be irrelevant. As head of product strategy at CNN, Jayesh Srivastava saw how using the wrong measures could derail design. "When I arrived here," he told us, "[the company] focused on measuring time spent on our website. The design team's mission was to design the service to have people *be better informed.* That's not the same thing as time on the site – although that's the metric that gets attention."

While time spent on the site was easy to measure and track, it didn't measure how well-informed CNN's viewers were. Nor did it tell the story of how CNN engaged and created value with its audience. Srivastava worried about the impact this approach might have on the CNN brand. "For a company whose mission is to be 'The Most Trusted Name in News,'" he said, "directing design decisions based on numeric website analytics, versus contextual data and feedback from actual people, is consequential and leads to a short-term quarterly focus."

At their best, numbers offer clarity, consistency, and statistical validity. At their worst, they shift focus away from value creation to value extraction, and obstruct innovation. When the numbers are made up, or measure the wrong things, in the wrong ways, at the wrong time, everybody loses.

Dehumanizing Design Work

The value extraction model also dehumanizes the work designers do.

According to Marshall Sitten, VP of service design at Citibank, numbers fail to capture the essence of design work, and discount – or entirely overlook – human experience. "Human experiences don't fit neatly into the linear and logical structure of spreadsheets, or bullets in a PowerPoint deck. Designers need to communicate and shape non-linear experiences that happen over time, and in different digital and physical spaces."

Dr. Emma Aiken-Klar saw how design work can be dehumanized. Aiken-Klar, an anthropologist and now head of her own innovation consulting firm, has spent her career applying qualitative research to design and innovation projects within the private and social sectors. A few years ago, she experienced a rude awakening when the design/innovation studio she was working for was acquired by a multinational software corporation.

Right away, the team was under pressure to do its work differently – not because of any change in project needs, but as a result of the parent company's accounting systems. "They couldn't account for important parts of the job, like having time to think before generating the final deliverable," she said. In this and many other ways, the quality of team members' work differed from the parent company's core software business, but senior management used the same tools to measure and manage both. Within two years, almost everyone on the team had left.

Design is not an assembly line, and design work does not lend itself to assembly-line measurement. Aiken-Klar experienced the challenge of managing design according to the accounting methods born of the efficiency-based value extraction model.

Distancing from Users

Under the extractive model of business, customers are also treated as assets to be exploited, not human beings.

After Sarah Drummond's company was taken over, she saw how spreadsheets drove decisions, and how human experience was forced to fit into discrete categories. Founder of the UK design studio Snook, she became chief digital officer at the multinational corporation that acquired the studio.

She was shocked at how financially driven the KPIs were. While Drummond was no stranger to the need to be profitable, "it was surprising to see the executive team drive *all* their decisions based on a single spreadsheet projected onto a wall. And [I was] fascinated to know that the tax year sets the rhythm of decision making, of what we value in business."

What's wrong with managing a business around the tax season and using spreadsheets to track progress? we asked. "The actual human experience," she replied, after a pause. "We try to mechanize human behavior and put it into a … binary way of working: User turns up for work, user works three and half hours, user has one hour lunch, user works another three and a half hours, user clocks off, user comes back to work. It's very robotic."

For Drummond, spreadsheets undermined leadership too. "When you are looking at spreadsheets, it's easy to find quick solutions to every problem," she said. "Basically, it's like taking plasticky plasters and putting them over top of problems." In doing so, you could slot every human problem, regardless of its individual context, into a predefined category. "I think that humans need to be loved and cared for, as opposed to being treated mechanistically," she said.

Many designers are shocked when they first encounter this paradigm. When companies claim to be "customer-centric," designers understand this language to mean that they are making things work better by researching, co-designing and testing. Yet they don't realize that their work will be judged according to KPIs that have little to do with customers as humans. The incongruity can lead to an uncomfortable sense of being gaslit.

Understanding the Business Model Bind

The Business Model bind is the result of different assumptions between managers and designers about the role of design. Much of this may originate in their training, rather than to personality or mindset differences: In the vast majority of business schools, extraction, measurement, and control are fundamental, while design schools focus more on making things through craft and creativity.

The tension generated by the Business Model bind is often concealed by blanket terms used by both managers and designers: customer-centricity, innovation, insights. However, these hold very different meanings in the minds of designers and managers. "A business analyst and a design researcher will both use the term 'insight,' but what they actually mean are entirely different things," Anthony Wolf, vice president of product development and innovation at hardware retailer Canadian Tire pointed out. These different meanings arise from different assumptions about value and values, the logic of business, and the role of design in strategy.

Value and Values

Across the private and public sectors, organizations have adopted design as a way to improve efficiency, to be more competitive, and to increase value to the organization, in terms of revenue, cost, and profit. Throughout the 2000s and 2010s, design was recognized and practiced for its value-generating advantages at blue chip companies like Procter & Gamble, IBM, Coca Cola, and Ford[3]; with governments and NGOs; and at academic institutions.

One of design's biggest – and perhaps most counterintuitive – proponents, global management consultancy McKinsey, claims that companies that embrace design correlate with "32 percentage points higher revenue growth and 56 per cent higher shareholder returns."[4] McKinsey's promotional literature proclaims how even in hard times, design offers a reliable and efficient way for companies to increase revenue.[5]

In this view, design is an instrument to drive revenue growth. But for those practicing design, their understanding extends beyond influencing consumers' next purchase. Designers' human-centered approach tunes them into users' emotional and social needs, and they believe that researching and designing will lead to something people find valuable, on the *user's* terms, rather than those of the business.

The promoters of design thinking peddle the illusion that the interests of users, of society, and of business are aligned, but this is far from always the case. "The working assumption that business interests and user interests are inherently aligned (they are often not) prevents designers from doing the work that would be more likely to bring those interests into alignment," tweeted Erika Hall, co-founder of Mule Design, in a twitter thread challenging the notion of placing an ROI on design.

Design is not just about pleasing users and promoting consumption. Many designers see their practice as a way to respond to social movements, such as #blacklivesmatter, #metoo, and climate activism, that have changed expectations around the role of private and public institutions in society. Among those we interviewed, there was a growing sense that simply applying design to win new customers and optimize your organization's efficiency is not enough.

These designers want to see their work positively influence the lives of individuals and the communities with whom they research and design. Mike Roy has spent the last 20 years working at leading design and technology firms such as Dubberly, MAYA and MURAL, where he now works as a senior product designer. "In some organizations, the notion of competition and winning is all important. And so 'We'll do whatever is required in order to win' becomes the norm," he said. "Whereas if you're cultivating empathy with design, then your attitude is 'Hey, let's offer something new to the world. We don't have to win. We just want to make things better for everybody.'"

Dori Tunstall, former dean of design at Ontario College of Art & Design University (OCADU), captured this dilemma in an interview (see Box, "What Designers Value"). Designers – and many managers – feel stuck between two irreconcilable demands: the pressure to maximize efficiency and value extraction, while responding to changing user needs and social movements.

**WHAT DESIGNERS VALUE
DORI TUNSTALL, FORMER DEAN, FACULTY OF
DESIGN, OCADU**

What we value is a form of prioritization. Implicit in creating things is a hierarchy, where we're saying, *this* is more important than *that*. We say we value things like democracy, sustainability, care, respect, and we can choose those things as more valuable than competition, extraction, excess, and harm. These are the kinds of experiences we want our children, or children's children's children, to have.

That prioritization process happens when we begin to create … objects or services or institutions.

The conundrum of the designer … is giving form to a set of values that might be in some ways misaligned with [their] own. That creates an internal tension, misalignment with what we believe the world *should* be doing. Just take sustainability, and assume that most managers are operating under a capitalist system, then there are things that are valued: Make it fast and efficient, right? Make it provide economic wealth. Profit [to] shareholders over better care for workers.

The conflict comes in the fact that there is an imposed set of values that are not contributing to either the flourishing of the planet or the flourishing of people, and even less a flourishing of the workers within the environment. That power that the designer has to create can begin to feel corrupted.

That's where you get demoralized. You need to pay a mortgage, to pay for a car, the need to provide education for your children, all those things force the designer to submit to others' values, which can make them feel trapped ... But one of the beautiful things that I loved when I was doing high-tech consulting is that you can actually transform organizations.

People don't understand that when I'm designing, I'm actually doing organizational transformation. By redesigning something like the intranet, we'll change the organization, oftentimes redefining the values of the organization.

So for me, this is where designers need to understand their power. You may not get it in year one, get to that place where you're really able to see the impact of what it is that you're doing. However, if you stick it out, whether you're designing an app or a poster – if you are being intentional about what you can change, then you can make an impact.

Then, all of a sudden, your understanding of what it is that you're doing in that organization shifts. Having clarity on where you can have an impact helps designers to articulate their value.

The Business Model bind is a symptom of this divergence in the meaning of value. We – designers and managers – are all part of a system that has an increasing wealth gap,[6] job dissatisfaction,[7] and accelerated social and environmental crises. Yet we continue to misuse design as a way to generate more short-term revenue, rather than more solutions to pressing problems that affect us all.

Efficiency and Product-Dominant Logic

Underpinning the different perspectives of managers and designers about value is a different type of logic: "product-dominant" logic versus "service-dominant" logic.

With roots in the classical and neoclassical economics of the nineteenth and twentieth centuries, product-dominant logic is the logic of standardization and efficiency. Under this logic, argued business professors Stephen Vargo and Robert Lusch in a classic 2004 paper, wealth in society was created by the acquisition of tangible products.[8]

As competition intensified through the twentieth century, and it became ever more challenging to differentiate products, two things happened. With fewer differentiating features, many companies focused on making products more cheaply and efficiently, as their primary performance drivers. Others sought to differentiate in other ways, by adding services and experiences.[9]

However, Vargo and Lusch argued that the very definition of value is evolving to a new, service-dominant model that dramatically alters an organization's operations, culture, and overall strategic outlook, to create mutual benefits for buyer and seller groups. The differences between the two models are summarized in Table 5.1.

At Polestar, the Volvo-owned electric car company, service designer Anya Earnest described how traditional "product logic" gets in the way of creating value with customers.

In the twentieth century, automakers manufactured and shipped automobiles with a focus on building in features – such as high-performance engines or interior trim – that could be manufactured and delivered efficiently. The company and its designers embedded value early in its development, and the company had limited engagement with users post-purchase because the product

Table 5.1 *Snapshot of 20th- and 21st-century business models, based on Vargo and Lusch (2004)*

20th Century Business Model	21st Century Business Model
Company manufactures and controls on their own terms	Value is delivered within customer context and networks
Company defines value	Customers define value
Transaction-oriented	Interaction-oriented
Designer involved up front	Designer involvement is ongoing
Profit-driven	Value-driven
Customers as targets	Customers as resources

Source: Vargo, S.L., & Lusch, R.F. (2004). Evolving to a new dominant logic for marketing. *Journal of Marketing*, 68(1), 1–17.

had already been manufactured and sold. Said Earnest, "Now we have app stores directly within vehicles. Suddenly we've gone from having a black box that only R+D can work with, to a system where we are constantly in contact with our customers and getting feedback in real time."

Advances in onboard computers in cars, offering everything from custom lighting and displays to boosts in horsepower and acceleration, enable customers to customize and adapt through an ongoing relationship with the company. Although customers are still buying a vehicle, the roles of the consumer and the designer have radically changed. "Now this is not a big thing if you have been working with the web or digital services, but in the car industry … it's mindblowing!"

The logic of product is different from the logic of service. Every service experience is idiosyncratic and individual, and while the company may deliver it, its *meaning*, and therefore its value, can only be created by the customer. To compete effectively in the twenty-first century, argued Vargo and Lusch, organizations' relationships with customers needed to extend far before and after the purchase transaction, and to account for more than efficiency and short-term profit. We saw a similar argument in chapter 4, with Prahalad and Ramaswamy's plea for a new paradigm that emphasized co-creation of value with customers.

Yet even in launching new products or responding to consumer trends, the implicit logic driving most managers remains as before: How do we exploit insight about customers to increase revenue and reduce costs? Variables that were valued under product-dominant logic, such as optimizing a factory to reduce labor costs, continue to dominate over the perspective of the end user.

For designers working in situ with front line staff and users, the disconnect between creating valuable experiences versus improving KPIs based on product logic can feel bewildering. "There was always this lens of efficiency, without thinking of the unintended consequences that efficiency can drive," said Bruno Silva, reflecting on his experiences at Mount Sinai Hospital in New York City. "When *we* worked on redesigning patient intake, *they* [hospital administration] were thinking about how to get the patients in and out the fastest. When we did the work, we realized that patients had different needs – but figuring out how we can get the patients in and out in a way that also leaves them satisfied with their treatment experience, or having the information they needed ... that was not the priority."

Design and Strategy: The Second Road

As we saw in chapter 1, design has moved beyond the realm of designing "things" – graphics and objects – to designing actions and environments. Yet many organizations have been unable or unwilling to respond to this fundamental shift.

In chapter 1, we discussed Richard Buchanan's Four Orders of Design. Buchanan also distinguished design as a mindset, expressing it as two roads (see Figure 5.1). The first road is about aesthetic improvements – colloquially, "toasters and posters." The

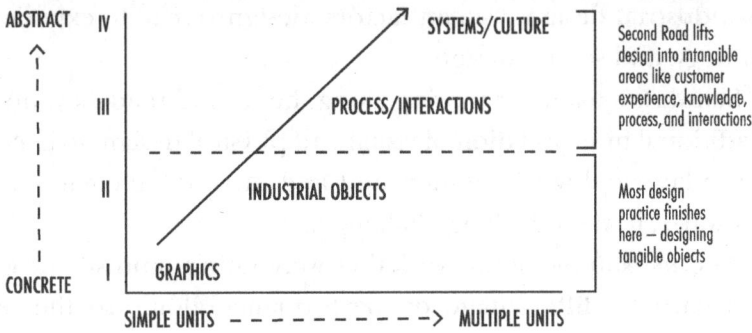

Figure 5.1 *The two roads of design. (Buchanan, 1992)*

second road is about the design of organizations' core structures and culture. Buchanan saw that organizations that embraced design, not as a set of tools but as a *mindset for understanding and shaping complicated systems*, fundamentally transformed how value is created.

When he decided to go in-house at a pharmaceutical and medical device corporation with a global presence and over 125,000 employees, Daniel Schwartz, a veteran design leader who had led teams at global design and innovation firms IDEO and SY Partners, was excited about working in such a large and well-resourced organization. Yet not long after the lab got off the ground, the team was laid off and the program canceled. A few weeks afterwards, in the wake of the news, we spoke with him about the rise and rapid collapse of design inside one of the world's largest multinationals.

Schwartz started by explaining how design initially evolved at the company and expanded its impact. "As the practice matured, we weren't just doing design in terms of brand design and packaging design," he told us. Design expanded into medical devices, pharmaceuticals, and supply chains, blending disciplines such as industrial design, human factors, design research, experience strategy, and service design.

Schwartz's team was moving along the second road: beyond the traditional interpretation of visual and physical design, to become a fundamental way to understand and drive value creation. For Schwartz, it was a thrilling challenge.

As one example of the work they were doing, a prosthetic knee was hard to differentiate on performance alone, so the team looked at the way the company serviced surgeons. Under the old-school model, hospital-based sales reps, or "consultants," would build close relationships with surgeons: walking with them to the surgical suite, recommending products, helping them select the right products, helping them with a question on a product. The downside was inventory management because the system meant that the consultants had to have a myriad of products on hand in case of need. Still, this was manageable – as long as most surgeries were done in large hospitals. But, as surgeries became dispersed across multiple centers, the old system became unwieldy.

Right away, Schwartz saw the potential for change. "WOW!" he exclaimed. "What an opportunity for service design to revolutionize!"

His excitement was quickly tempered by the reality of applying design within a large organization. Since the commercial team owned the problem, they came up with quick fixes based on the existing, flawed, business model: incentive plans, technologies like RFID, and optimizing placement of products.

Schwartz took a different approach: He went into the field to see what was going on. He discovered that this was not an *inventory* problem, as the commercial team was assuming, but a *human burden* problem: "How do we make [sales consultants'] life better? It's going at the problem through a different door." He added, "I have the belief – I guess it's a kind of naïve, idealistic view of designers – that if I solve *that* problem, the value will follow."

The program with hospital consultants was not implemented, and after a series of organizational changes and new senior leadership, the lab was shuttered. What remained was only the first road of design: tangible products that fit clearly within commercial operations: physical medical devices, digital technology, and so on. "People are doing good old-fashioned consumer design, like old school ... branding and packaging. To [management], that's value," he said.

As a designer, Schwartz had discovered that he had a different viewpoint on strategy from the status quo. He didn't just look to internal departments to see how things could be improved based on the company's past, but instead thought about the context of consultants working in hospitals. He began to reimagine the interactions and processes from *their* perspective, rather than the perspective of the corporation.

He shrugged. The experience, he said, "seems to fit the narratives of financial engineering and optimizing organizations." It certainly showed how, in some organizations, the second road of design may be further off than their corporate messaging would imply.

Loosening the Business Model Bind

As we noted earlier, the invisibility of the Business Model bind can leave designers feeling gaslit. However, some design leaders are making progress, taking on the bind in ways that improve the success of design teams and help organizations generate more valuable experiences. They take the initiative and expose tradeoffs between the extractive model and value creation; they learn to challenge quantitative measures; they use numbers to their advantage; and they engage managers with user stories.

Designers Define the Trade-Offs

For some design leaders, the work of designers includes proactively understanding business value *and* user value, to see where the tradeoffs are.

Dr. Linus Schaff has spent the last decade at Volkswagen Group, where he started its Service Design Lab as part of his PhD work. He now works in transformation roles, and sees the role of the designer as integral to transitioning to the future. "Organizations," he told us, "are shifting designers, to learn how to quantify ... the business impact their value creation would bring." This, he argued, changes the discussion dramatically: Designers will have to understand *both* value to the user and business value.

But, since the best-fulfilled user needs might not translate into the highest business value, there is often a tradeoff. Schaff argued that understanding such tradeoffs is good for design. "Designers," he said, "will be compromising between these two tensions – but *they*, the designer, will define this compromise."

While there are many examples of designers conforming to the value extraction business model by adding quantitative data to human experiences, or by dashboarding journeys, the notion of the designer defining tradeoffs places them in a different position. Rather than adopting the dominant extractive model of the past, designers can introduce a new business model that accounts for human and social value.

In the telco story that opened this chapter, the design team explicitly exposed the tradeoff between transparency and the existing business model. They created three different scenarios; within each scenario, the team showed the potential impacts on human experience – such as trust – against business impacts, such as margins. This helped internal stakeholders to understand the impacts, particularly in the longer term, of obfuscating pricing versus clarifying incentives for returning customers.

Challenge the Measures

For frustrated designers, the message from Snook's Sarah Drummond is not to be obnoxious, but to maintain a collegial approach. Drummond sets clear expectations, with project initiation sheets that describe intended outcomes. Drummond recommends looking at clients and stakeholders as "a mate you can take for a beer and have real conversations with," as opposed to being righteous and indignant.

Successful designers don't just act nice: They demonstrate the limits of traditional data and are realistic about what they can accomplish. "Traditional data and KPIs are like using a metal detector on the beach," TELUS' Judy Mellett, now vice-president of Product and Platforms, Channels and Customer Experience at LifeLabs, told us. "You have an idea that something is happening, but it is completely obscured from view."

Using quantitative data, Mellett creates a "doorway to context" that highlights the fact that a problem exists, providing an opportunity to go deeper. To accomplish this, she initiates direct conversations that demonstrate the limits of quantitative measures: She asks questions about why a phenomenon is happening, shows what is unknown, and then leverages design to provide contextual insights.

Shift Perspectives with User Stories

Ultimately, numbers and ethnographic data do the same thing: They tell a story. Many managers see quantitative data as "objective," but that's a fallacy. What happens to your heart rate if you look at a red line showing your investments losing value? Just as your emotions are engaged, so a CEO's emotions are engaged by a profit and loss statement – after all, their job depends on it.

But the superpower of qualitative research is its ability to engage executives in ways no financial statement can. As design practitioners, we have seen this over and over: Simply by quoting users, or

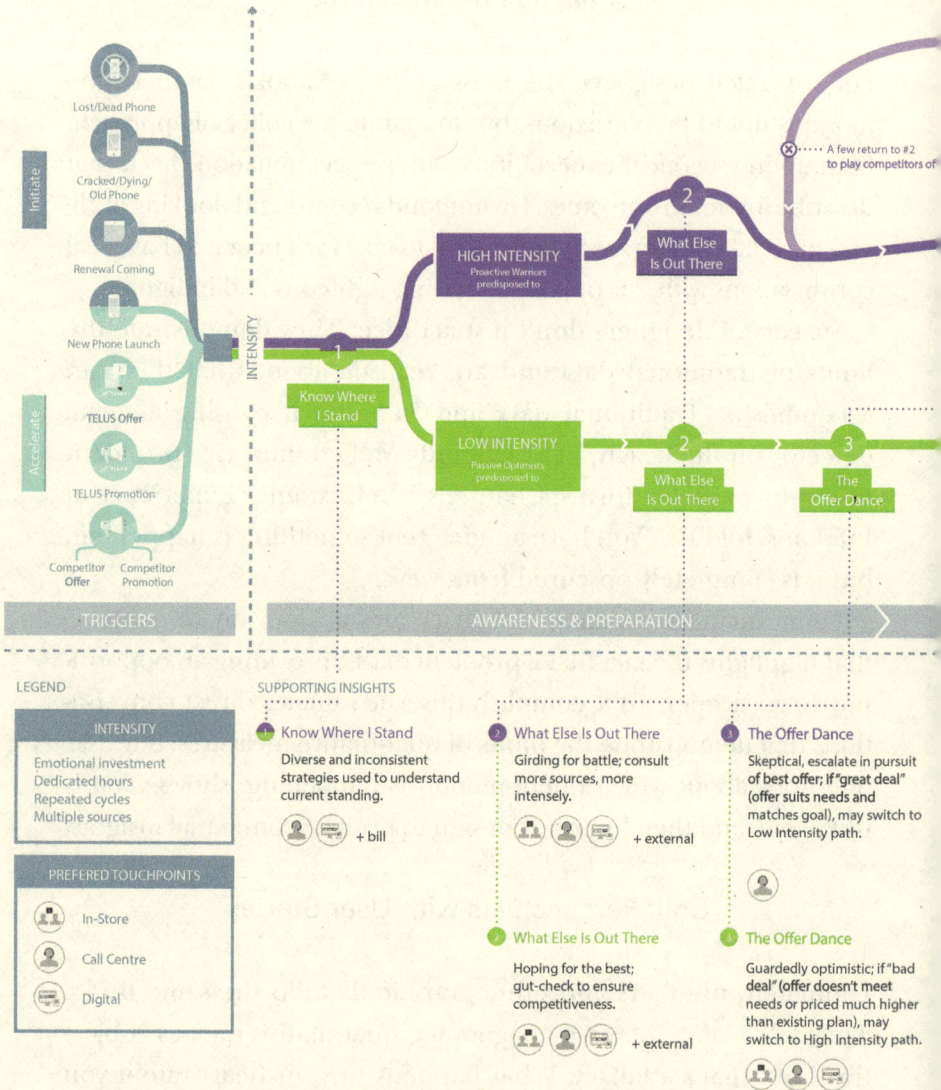

Figure 5.2 *An Experience Map highlights customers' pain points and preferences. (Bridgeable, 2016)*

Lost/Dead Phone

Cracked/Dying/
Old Phone

Renewal Coming

New Phone Launch

TELUS Offer

TELUS Promotion

Competitor   Competitor
Offer   Promotion

Initiate

Accelerate

INTENSITY

HIGH INTENSITY
Proactive Warriors
predisposed to

1
Know Where
I Stand

2
What Else
Is Out There

A few return to #2
to play competitors of

LOW INTENSITY
Passive Optimists
predisposed to

2
What Else
Is Out There

3
The
Offer Dance

TRIGGERS

AWARENESS & PREPARATION

LEGEND

SUPPORTING INSIGHTS

INTENSITY

Emotional investment
Dedicated hours
Repeated cycles
Multiple sources

PREFERED TOUCHPOINTS

In-Store

Call Centre

Digital

1 Know Where I Stand

Diverse and inconsistent
strategies used to understand
current standing.

+ bill

2 What Else Is Out There

Girding for battle; consult
more sources, more
intensely.

+ external

2 What Else Is Out There

Hoping for the best;
gut-check to ensure
competitiveness.

+ external

3 The Offer Dance

Skeptical, escalate in pursuit
of best offer; if "great deal"
(offer suits needs and
matches goal), may switch to
Low Intensity path.

3 The Offer Dance

Guardedly optimistic; if "bad
deal" (offer doesn't meet
needs or priced much higher
than existing plan), may
switch to High Intensity path.

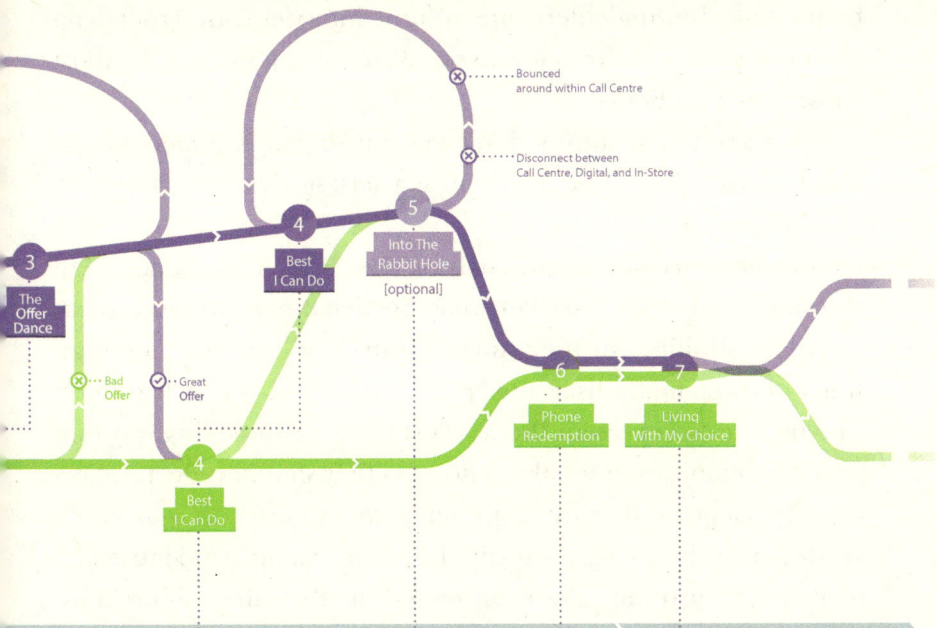

Bounced
around within Call Centre

Disconnect between
Call Centre, Digital, and In-Store

3 — The Offer Dance

4 — Best I Can Do

5 — Into The Rabbit Hole [optional]

6 — Phone Redemption

7 — Living With My Choice

Bad Offer

Great Offer

4 — Best I Can Do

ENGAGEMENT & COMPLETION

CONFIRMATION

Best I Can Do
Fight seen as worthwhile, even when short of desired goal.

Into the Rabbit Hole [optional]
Frustration runs high as customer is forced to fight for what they feel they were promised.

Phone Redemption
Excited to get and set up new phone.

Living With My Choice
Looking for validation online and/or in first bill; if wrong plan, high overage, or dissatisfied with device, may lead to feeling exploited and can trigger shift back onto High Intensity path to resolve.

+ bill

Best I Can Do
Pleased that it's over with.

better still, showing video clips of user interviews, designers can elicit every reaction from joy, to shock, to misery, in even the most conservative audience.

The reason? Executives don't get out much. Numbers create distance from users, treating them as assets; stories create intimacy and insight.

The methods of design, such as the Telus Experience Map shown in Figure 5.2, User Personas, Service Blueprints and so on, are the scaffolding of user stories. Many who are new to design think of these methods as the "point" of design, but they are not: The point is to represent the user's story in a compelling way that gets the organization to take action. So they should reflect subjective experience – how the experience *feels* to the user – as much as the stages the user goes through. In the example in Figure 5.2, feelings of frustration are represented in labels like falling "Into the Rabbit Hole."

So let them hear the voice of the user to reorient themselves towards what they value. Use it everywhere you can, and use it again. See every interaction with internal teams as a chance to shift perspectives towards user value. Then you can rightly argue that "it's not *us*, the designers, who are telling you this. It's your customers, on whom the future of this organization depends."

The Business Model bind, and the measures that go with it, are rooted in a history that is evolving, and, like all evolutionary processes, progress is slow but inexorable. The old paradigm about value will disappear, though not overnight; designers need to retain a clear-eyed commitment to change and help accelerate its demise.

6 The Scope Bind

Design is typically compartmentalized in organizations, ostensibly to protect nas-cent thinking, but in reality to protect the organization from ideas that are too radical. It is treated as a form of play, trivialized, and confined to minor product improvements. Designers need to address the cultural factors that restrict design from achieving its full potential.

When MindLab, the Danish government's design lab, was founded in 2002, its founding director, Mikkel B. Rasmussen, stated its purpose as "throwing a hand grenade at the bureaucracy."[1] Four years later, an internal evaluation concluded that, as a process catalyst – a facilitator of brainstorming workshops – and a project initiator, MindLab had proven its value. But, according to Christian Bason, its director from 2007 to 2016, this wasn't the whole story: Mind-Lab's activities were "a little bit too superficial, too short to have a deeper impact."

After considering the alternatives – including permanently shuttering the lab – the Ministry of Business Affairs decided to scale it up, in partnership with the Ministry of Taxation and the Ministry of Employment. MindLab became a locus for user-centered design of policy, extending its involvement in projects beyond the kick-off stage to become a long-term partner with government departments. In addition, it shifted its focus to addressing wicked problems in society. With an annual budget of €1.2 million, it was a major initiative by the Danish government.

By 2011, Bason and the MindLab team felt that the lab could play a much larger role, to help bring about real change in government and society. In a 2012 article, Bason and co-author Helle Vibeke Carstensen wrote:

> Sustainable innovation – if that was truly to be MindLab's objective – would not happen via isolated projects. Innovation should lead to lasting public value across multiple bottom lines. In MindLab's experience, this required ... even deeper, longer-term, top-level engagement.[2]

MindLab's core approach was to bring a citizen's perspective to government as the basis for better ideas about policies and programs. In its new, expanded role, it took on two major initiatives: organizational change and exploring new policy directions.

Ultimately, though, MindLab's effort to bring about fundamental change failed. The lab was shut down in 2018 and replaced by a digital task force.

There were many reasons for MindLab's demise. However, the lab's distinct culture from the bureaucracy, the challenge of bringing innovation to government policy, shifts in prevailing power structures, and the difficulty in measuring the results of its projects all played a part. In its attempt to broaden its activities beyond workshop facilitation, it ultimately became a victim of the Scope bind.

The Scope Bind

Double binds work together to limit the impact of design in organizations. The Scope bind is often the most tangible result: the simultaneous acceptance and rejection of design, when it is tolerated as harmless, if occasionally useful, fun. At the same time, it is kept firmly in a box, sealed off from anything of strategic importance.

Experiencing the Scope Bind

Though it's true to say that design is widely accepted in business and government, that's a far cry from saying that its capabilities are fully utilized.

Reframing problems by challenging the fundamentals is a core design skill. Apart from frustrating and demotivating designers, the Scope bind cuts them off from this critical phase in the process. It leads to innovations that may be coherent but strategically wrong; that miss crucial insights and opportunities to transform markets; or that stress continuity where radical change is called for.

The Scope bind is at work where design is treated as a fringe activity, commonly as decoration or as a form of corporate play. It is also seen where designers are briefed to develop incremental innovations, but never allowed to deviate or question the underlying strategies.

Scope can enable or constrain action by what it includes in the frame. When it comes to redesigning value, scope can fundamentally constrain teams' ability to solve problems, by ignoring underlying conditions and root causes. By decoupling "design problems" from structure, history, and consideration of systemic oppression, larger social and environmental concerns can be glossed over, and design reduced to treating superficial symptoms.[3]

Design as Decoration

Design is often seen as just a way to "make things pretty." In chapter 1, we discussed how design has expanded from its traditional territory into strategy and wicked problems. Even apparently minor product or service changes can have much deeper repercussions – for example, to make a "safe" automobile, one needs to address fundamental issues about safety (What is "safe"? What level of safety, or unsafety, is acceptable?), user context, comfort, convenience, distribution channels, supply chain, and a host of other factors.[4] For designers to address such problems, they need a deep understanding of users, context, and strategy. Yet many organizations don't seem to have gotten the message.

In one case, a client asked an innovation consultancy if they could "borrow" a designer for a couple of hours to make some templates and slides. The designer in question was highly skilled, had a combined MBA/MDes, and later went on to advise the Cabinet office for a provincial government. "The role of the designer was seen as someone who could make things look pretty. It was about the veneer and not the substance. They didn't want to pay for the experience and thinking, the skill to facilitate with people, or to tangibilize the outputs," said the frustrated CEO of the consultancy. "Designers are more than just making something look good, right? They actually bring a depth of capabilities to the table," said another design leader. When design is relegated to prettification, the result is a glossy veneer on poorly thought-out ideas.

Corporate Play

"If I need a puppet show, I'll go to those guys [designers]," said a leader at a global consulting firm. In what has become known as "design theater," designers are seen as the organization's clowns.

A senior designer in the public sector captured this neatly, at a discussion on design in organizations. "We're the lunchtime entertainment," she said, rolling her eyes. Design workshops were often organized as a lunchtime activity at all-day offsite meetings, as a relief from the heavy work of ploughing through PowerPoints and spreadsheets. It wasn't that their colleagues disliked design – in some ways, they liked it *too* much, as a source of harmless fun. But it seemed that fun and work were mutually exclusive. By definition, if you were having fun, you must not be working; and if you were working, you most certainly should not be having fun.

Unfortunately, designers themselves have often exploited this image of the designer as clown. Design firms and consultants have oversold design as a form of magic: Just wave a user persona and an empathy map, and *presto!*, disruptive innovation. Workshops that emphasize the "play" side of design, and exercises like the spaghetti exercise – in which participants compete to build the tallest structure using dry spaghetti, tape, string and a marshmallow – make it all look easy and fun.

When he was introducing design at RBC, Peter Chow started by using the spaghetti tower exercise. At the time, he saw it as an activity with a serious lesson: Show participants how to collaborate, and how iteration is "way faster, way better, and way more effective." But the unintentional takeaway was that design was frivolous.

"It drove me crazy," said Chow. Participants were learning how to build spaghetti towers but missing the bigger lesson about the value of design in business. "All everyone wanted to talk about was how high their spaghetti tower was, or what innovative way they figured out to game the system."

"I'm glad you had fun," Chow would respond, trying – futilely – to redirect participants to the point of the exercise. It made design look silly, and in a large, conservative organization like a bank, this could be fatal. "We retired the spaghetti tower activity," said Chow.

Design theater is little more than an attention-getting tactic. It can overwhelm the less sexy, but essential, aspects of design: observing and interviewing users, analyzing and clustering data, reframing problems, methodically capturing all aspects of user experience, mapping systems and processes, and iterating endlessly – sometimes ad nauseam. The practice of design demands intense focus, persistence, curiosity, and reflectiveness, and spaghetti towers do little to show this. In fact, they show the opposite, tapping into the preconceived image of designers as magicians.

Incremental Innovation

As we saw in chapter 3, companies that use design purely for incremental innovation are missing out. Most organizations initially adopt design to improve user experience, by enhancing the usability or aesthetics of their products, or by improving the service journey. Some have used it to develop disruptive new products or services – but few adopt design as a route to better strategies.

Even when organizations appreciate designers' thinking skills, they fail to use them. "There are companies that hire a lot of designers based on their skill sets of being creative, productive, or logical thinkers," André Nogueira, associate faculty of Design Knowledge at the Johns Hopkins School of Nursing, and CEO of Leap, told us, "[But] then they don't get to be in positions of authority." It's hard to escape the box: Have fun, make things look good – but don't question whether the things should exist in the first place.

In a 2015 interview, PepsiCo's CEO Indra Nooyi extolled the benefits of design in coming up with better snack products and distributing them through vending machines – but, when questioned about their impact on obesity and public health, had little to say about any role for design in creating better outcomes for users and society.[5]

"Oftentimes, people who've never worked with designers before don't really understand what value they're bringing, and what they can actually do," said Ophelia Chiu, vice president, of strategic innovation at Memorial Sloan Kettering in New York. Without a solid understanding of design, its countless iterations and speculative thinking can make it appear an expensive, time-consuming way of solving problems.

For Chiu, design is falling short of its potential. "How do we actually think about elevating the understanding of what design actually is? And how do we think about where it's at? Because design would be wonderful contributing to a much broader set of projects."

It's not wrong to think that designers are good at making nice slides, running cool workshops, or improving service delivery. But designers are capable of so much more. Using designers to prettify slides is like taking an aspirin for a brain tumor: It may help a little with the symptoms, but it won't change what needs changing.

A notable exception was the Australian Tax Office, where design grew out of strategy. Originally introduced in the early 2000s, the program emerged from "strategic conversations," an approach to strategy that emphasized collaborative dialogue and visualization. Useful as these conversations were, they eventually ran out of steam. As John Body, a principal advocate of design at the ATO, said in an interview, "We thought, 'the strategy's really interesting and we've had a few breakthroughs, but is it changing anything for people on the ground?'" Design brought a *complementary* lens to strategy, both as a way of making a difference to the experience of taxpayers, and of shifting the organization's culture to a more taxpayer-friendly stance.

The effect on the ATO's culture was dramatic, flipping it from an organization notorious for its hostile and predatory attitude to taxpayers, to a user- (i.e., taxpayer-) friendly, learning organization. Body found that this new way of thinking came as a dose of reality to the ATO: "You suddenly realize that people don't jump out of bed every morning thinking 'I'm a taxpayer and I'm going to pay my tax today.'" Used properly, design can transform both strategy *and* culture.

DAVID'S DESIGN JOURNEY

David is Teaching Professor Emeritus at the Peter B. Gustavson School of Business, University of Victoria. He started his career in marketing with consumer goods giant Unilever in London, UK. Moving into new product management, he found himself excited by the task of deeply understanding consumers and developing products to meet their needs.

A passion for teaching led him to academia, where, he felt, he could freely explore ideas with students. When he joined the Rotman School of Management in the late 1990s as a marketing professor, Dean Roger Martin was talking about design in business. In design, he saw echoes of the best parts of his previous career: dealing with ambiguous, challenging problems; understanding users and their context. But in asking fundamental questions, and in providing its own methods to develop intuition, he found that design was far ahead of the work he had been doing at Unilever. He decided to pivot away from marketing and devote his career to design.

The decision led him to teach business courses at design schools around the world while still exploring design at Rotman. As he immersed himself in this new milieu, he was struck by the creativity and energy of design students – a marked contrast from the business world he knew.

In his first class at TU Delft in the Netherlands, a design student asked a pointed question that took him aback. "What's all this fuss about growth in business? Why do businesses have to grow?" The student followed up with examples of companies where growth was a secondary consideration: Other goals like doing good for society, or providing its owners with a consistent, steady income, took precedence.

A question like this would never have been asked at Rotman, where growth was an unspoken article of faith. He knew he had found his tribe, one that was willing to ask those uncomfortable fundamental questions that had no easy answers. Published in 2018, his book *Design Thinking at Work* dealt with the tensions designers faced in organizations.

With a deep commitment to social and environmental sustainability, the Gustavson School, where he moved a few years later, was very different from Rotman. He launched the MBA in Sustainable Innovation and worked on the Gustavson Brand Trust Index (GBTI), a scorecard of consumers' trust in brands, based in part on the values each brand stood for.

But it still felt wrong. The GBTI, and the larger idea of "sustainable business," seemed to promote a Pollyanna world, where

free markets would take care of everything, and the interests of
the business world were identical to those of society: Nothing fundamental had to change. Even at this unique business school, the
iconoclastic spirit he saw in the design community was missing. In
writing this book, he saw a path forward, through design, that did
not shirk the difficult questions.

Understanding the Scope Bind

As we have seen, design has been sold – indeed, oversold – to the
business community as a panacea for a wide variety of ills.

Most organizations have more than one reason for adopting
design. Of course, they all want innovation. Some want incremental innovation: to tweak their products or services, to align
them better with customer experience, and gain a competitive
advantage. Others, seeing changes in society and shifts in their
competitive environment, look for disruptive innovation – though
they typically back off when they realize that this may mean disrupting their current culture and power structures. Too often,
though, they fall in love with the trappings of design theater: the
sticky notes, the Nerf balls, and the playful energy.

The resulting trivialization of design causes intense frustration
among designers. "Someone's done a weekend course," said one,
"and all of a sudden, they're doing co-design ... design is not a
weekend hobby. Designers are actually people that have skills, and
we need to respect those skills."

In practice, the overselling of design gives rise to two barriers,
one of which seems inevitable, the other inexcusable. The inevitable one is cultural resistance; the inexcusable one is ignorance.

The Organizational Culture Iceberg

Design can be countercultural in organizations – often, it *has* to be that way if it's to make a difference – and this can isolate it from the mainstream.

In 2018, Kimberley Elsbach and Ileana Stigliani dug into studies of design thinking and organizational culture. Both are professors in business schools – Elsbach at University of California, Davis, and Stigliani at Imperial College London – though Stigliani has a background in design. After an exhaustive search, they found that design thinking thrived in cultures that were *already* defined by collaboration and experimentation, but tended to struggle where productivity, performance, and silos dominated. In other words, design thinking did best where it was needed least.

Culture is mostly hidden from plain sight. Josina Vink has been thinking about organizational culture and design for some time and has a good deal to say about how design might transform cultures. Vink, an associate professor at The Oslo School of Architecture and Design, is "bilingual" in design and business, with both an extensive background as a service designer and a PhD in business administration, service design and health systems.

In a 2019 talk in Toronto,[6] Vink quoted Robert M. Pirsig's classic 1974 book *Zen and the Art of Motorcycle Maintenance*.[7] The quote reveals a great deal about designers' propensity to question underlying assumptions, and is worth repeating here:

If a factory is torn down but the rationality which produced it is left standing, then that rationality will simply produce another factory. If a revolution destroys a systematic government, but the systematic patterns of thought that produced that government are left intact, then those patterns will repeat themselves in the succeeding government. There's so much talk about the system. And so little understanding.

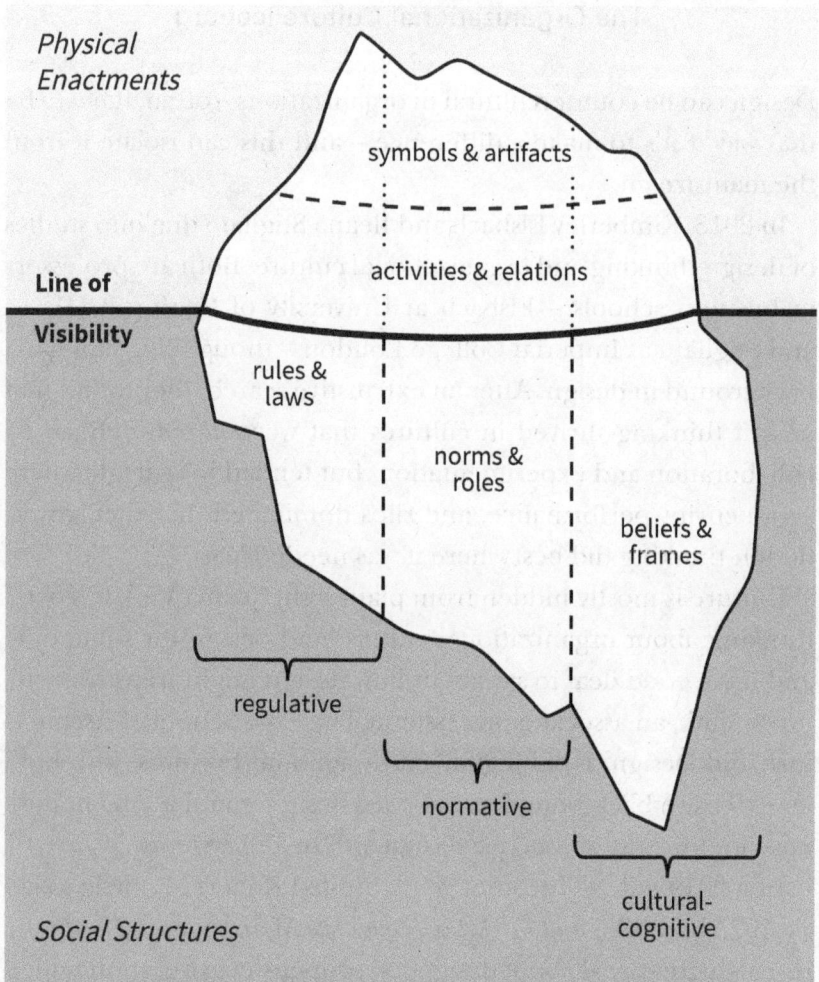

Figure 6.1 *Vink's iceberg model of organizational culture. (Josina Vink)*

"We are entrenched in ways of working that reinforce each other," claimed Vink. Yet, while some of these work patterns are visible, the cultural structures that underlie them are not. As shown in Figure 6.1, it's like an iceberg, where we see the external symbols of culture, not its foundations.

Vink's model helps explain some of the friction designers encounter in organizations. Vink identifies the visible part of culture in four physical enactments: symbols, artifacts, activities, and relations. These are supported, and shaped, by invisible institutional pillars: invisible rules, norms, and beliefs that lie underneath the surface. Implicitly, if you challenge the visible part, you are threatening the foundations.

Icebergs are inevitable, and, if you run into them, destructive. Yet perhaps an even more appropriate metaphor is the human body's immunity system.[8] Once design, like an alien virus, identifies itself by challenging the visible parts of culture, organizational antibodies – hitherto invisible – rally to destroy it. However, if design has been sanctioned from the top, they may not be able to eradicate it. Instead, they isolate it, to protect the status quo.

Ignorance and Confusion

The inexcusable reason – because organizations ought to know what they are taking on – for the Scope bind is misunderstanding of design.

The trope of the "elite designer," who, seemingly magically, comes up with wild ideas that transform everyday life, is alive and well in our culture. With more than a touch of arrogance, fashion designer Alexander McQueen once said, "I find beauty in the grotesque, like most artists. I have to force people to look at things." Industrial designer Philippe Starck said that his duty as a designer was to be "subversive, ethical, ecological, political, humorous." He didn't say strategic. McQueen's and Starck's ideas may lead to interesting aesthetics, but most companies would consider them a far cry from strategy.

What these clichés don't recognize is that design, even in its more artistic versions, is less about inspiration than about perspiration. As Jeanne Liedtka of the University of Virginia's Darden

School put it, looking to a genius like Steve Jobs as an example of how to do design is like looking to Moses for the best way to cross a river.[9] Design, like every field, has its prodigies, but they tell us little about the discipline of innovation.

Liedtka goes on to say that "design thinking gives us the ability to [innovate] in the form of a reliable set of processes and tools. Though it sounds mysterious, design thinking is just another approach to problem solving, an especially effective one if your goal is innovation."

But Liedtka's message glosses over the "mysterious" part, the *way* designers solve problems. Everyone wants to innovate, but the Scope bind arises from the way designers go about it.

How do designers innovate? They speculate. They look for unexpected connections. They go back and forth, rather than take the shortest route to problem solving. They alternate between abstract ideas and concrete expression.

This can come as a surprise to managers. As the health insurance design leader we met in chapter 3 argued, creativity "in the right place" is tolerated, but not in senior management. For Ross, you had to create options – to speculate on possibilities – before making choices, but her management colleagues instead tended to narrow down on what they already knew. "If you're the person in the room that wants to throw out a hypothesis or go abstract, there's this huge impact on your credibility, because people look at you as somehow distracted from the topic."

Because design has been sold so aggressively, it is seen as a signal to outsiders that you are serious about innovation. At Mount Sinai Hospital, Bruno Silva commented on how some institutions adopt design because it was a shiny object: "It's the coolest thing to do, and they want design thinking, but they don't really know how to use it."

"You don't know how many meetings I was pulled into, for funding or whatever," he added, "that I would just go in [to show that] we have a designer in the group." Dazzled by the design's sparkle, organizations that overlook its substance are bound to be disappointed.

Loosening the Scope Bind

The Scope Bind undermines design by boxing it in. Not only are designers frustrated, but the restrictions inevitably lead to a self-fulfilling prophecy: Designers will do little more than make things look good, and will fail to transform strategy. The designers we spoke to looked to loosen the Scope bind by addressing the culture head-on – i.e., by redesigning it – by relying on top management, by building legitimacy, and by taking advantage of serendipity.

Redesign the Culture

It may seem difficult, but it is possible to redesign an organization's culture.

When Elsbach and Stigliani discovered that design thinking did best in organizational cultures that already had attributes of design, they also found that cultures could be influenced by using specific design methods. For example, experimentation and prototyping could help develop a culture of openness to failure. Furthermore, they argued, the physical artifacts and emotional experiences produced by design could serve as powerful objects of reflection on organizational culture – in other words, sticky notes, empathy maps, and journey maps could be commandeered to promote cultures that were design friendly.

For Josina Vink, the iceberg is not an immovable object – quite the contrary, they see social structures as the "materials" of service design, key leverage points for intervening in a social system and changing its behavior. Design methods, Vink argues, can reshape employees' mental models through *sensing surprise* by exposing existing mental models, *perceiving multiples* by bringing out alternative models, and *embodying alternatives* by physically testing different ways of working.[10]

Can we really redesign a culture? These ideas are seductive, but they don't ring true. Examples of organizations that have successfully transformed their culture – *really* transformed it – through design are rare.

As we saw earlier, the Australian Tax Office might have qualified when design was first introduced – but design has waxed and waned there with changes in leadership. We asked some experts for examples. They too were stumped, but one name eventually came up: IBM.

In the 2010s, most of IBM's business came from its traditional products: conventional hardware, software, and services. As technology advanced ever more rapidly and streaming services became available, the company's future was looking ever more shaky. Revenues and share prices began to decline.

In 2010, Phil Gilbert's company Lombardi Software, based in Austin, Texas, was acquired by IBM. Gilbert was asked to recreate at IBM whatever Lombardi magic was making customers love their product. That magic was design, but not in its usual corporate form: Design infused every aspect of Lombardi, from sales to marketing to finance.

In 2012, Gilbert founded IBM Design. He recruited 1,500 designers from top schools like Stanford, Carnegie Mellon, the Rhode Island School of Design, and Parsons School of Design – not a trivial task, since IBM's image in the design community harked back to that *1984* ad, as a slow-moving behemoth – and set about reforming the company around design. The designers were distributed across the company's product teams, and worked alongside customers at 24 design studios around the world.

IBM also set about training its workforce in design thinking – not to turn them into designers, but to learn what designers were doing, and how to work effectively with design mindsets and methodologies. All senior managers took the training from the beginning, and the program has been spread steadily across the company over the past decade. The IBM Design philosophy is based on building bonds through care and craft, being a medium between mankind and machine, and making the design ethos palpable in everything the company produces.[11]

Given IBM's massive scale – in 2022, the company had almost 350,000 employees – instilling design across the culture is a daunting task. But the company, with full support of senior management, appears fully committed to this path. Shifting culture is far from easy, but if a Goliath like IBM can pull it off, it's a possibility open to any organization.

Untying from the Top Down

Design programs that survive in organizations almost always have unequivocal, sustained support from the top: a sponsor on the executive team, if not the CEO themselves, who is willing to put their reputation on the line for it.

At Ontario Digital Services, design leader Shannah Segal was working to convince her organization through experience, but she needed strong support – and a degree of luck. After extensive internal consultation, the Ontario Government passed the Simpler, Faster, Better Services Act. setting out principles for public-sector organizations, the first of which is that *the design and implementation of digital services should be user-centered.* The Act was followed in 2021 by the Ontario Digital Service Standard, and the Digital First Assessment, under which teams across the government are required to have their digital project assessed by ODS for compliance with the standard.

But even in the wake of these changes, acceptance of design was inconsistent across the government. As Segal saw it, design's path towards full acceptance unfolded in three phases: introduction, acceptance, and autonomy. Though design tended to be trivialized at the beginning, it was taken more seriously as it became more broadly accepted.

Segal's experience with the Ontario Government's supportive legislation showed how top-down mandates could force broad acceptance of design. However, it is important not to become too dependent on orders from the top. In both the public and private sectors, rapid turnover in leadership undermines support for design. The task is to take advantage of early support to put in place mechanisms, like the Digital Service Standard, that head off the Scope bind before it sets in.

Building Legitimacy

Hard as this may be for designers to accept, design has no inherent "right" to be at the strategy table.

In a 2015 paper, Ingo Rauth, Lisa Carlgren, and Maria Elmquist found that designers establish design thinking in organizations by "legitimizing" it. But this was not an instantaneous process. "Legitimacy," they argued, "is built individually, over time."[12]

Rauth and his colleagues identified five legitimization strategies. The first was *demonstrating design's usefulness*, by creating internal success stories and measuring project-specific outcomes. Designers also worked to *mesh design with organizational culture*, by including stakeholders, such as union members. Since design is fundamentally experiential, *convincing others through experience*, such as by participating in workshops, was an important part of legitimization. Designers also sought legitimacy by *creating physical spaces and artifacts*, such as a physical space devoted to design thinking, and training and advertising material.

Finally, designers *established ambassador networks* of senior management and employees who have participated in workshops. Ambassador networks could be established, too, by fostering collaboration with other units – an example of this is MindLab's focus on recruiting "nice" people, as we saw in chapter 4.

When Peter Chow abandoned spaghetti towers at RBC, he replaced the activity with Rauth, Carlgren, and Elmquist's first legitimization strategy, demonstrating design's usefulness, by developing "use-cases" to illustrate the value of design in areas that were directly connected to the business.

One thing that caught the team's attention was the chaos and disruption that happened in an office area when several teleconference meetings were going on at the same time.

As often happens in design projects, it was the framing of the problem that mattered, and simple, inexpensive fixes could trump more complex high-tech approaches. When you observed employees, it became obvious that they were having difficulties with multiple Zoom calls happening at the same time in an open-plan office. The solution, too, was obvious. "We [had] the world's best technology when it comes to ergonomics, seats, webcams, docking stations," said Chow, "and then we realized the most important things were headphones."

Chow and his team used this case, and others like it, to illustrate the power of design: Though the solutions they came up with were simple, the real magic of design was not in problem solving, but in problem *finding*. Observing behavior – the work environment, and how employees responded to it – on a small scale offered many more insights than traditional approaches like employee surveys, or throwing technology at a problem.

"Now," said Chow, "instead of showing them a spaghetti tower, we showed them, hey, look, we brought back fifteen people, here's all the learnings ... And then, from that, we started making strategic decisions. So we removed the theatrics, there's no more fun and games." The new approach sent a clear message to the organization: design was serious business.

Taking Advantage of Serendipity

Every now and again, a project pops up that can give designers the opportunity to shine.

Like Chow, Segal and her ODS colleagues took advantage of the COVID pandemic. When the Ontario government shut down its offices in March 2020, the ODS design team was – accidentally – ready. "Everybody basically just put their computers in their bags and left," she said. But the design team was already accustomed to using tools like Miro, Teams, and Zoom. While others were struggling to learn how to use the software, and busy connecting up webcams and microphones, the design team didn't miss a beat, and ODS's reputation across the Ontario government grew as a result. This led to more project work and greater experience with design across the government.

The shutdown of MindLab served as a pointed lesson for design labs everywhere: Pay as much attention to your position and fit in your organization as you do to your design work. Bureaucracies, a reality in both public and private sectors, tend to resist having hand grenades thrown at them. But designers have shown that a keen awareness of organizational culture can point the way to loosening the Scope bind, and demonstrating design's full potential.

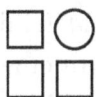

7 The Epistemology Bind

Managers and designers come from very different traditions and have very different ways of knowing. The assumptions that underlie positivist, quantitative thinking are rarely questioned in organizations. These assumptions, with their origins in colonialism and a bias for financialization, must be addressed if we are to solve the massive problems facing the world. Designers play a key role in confronting this conventional way of thinking.

Before joining Ireland's VHI, Lorna Ross was a designer at Accenture, a global consulting firm.

"We were having a lot of conversations about automation in the workforce, and the future of work, and the displacement of people from technology. There were a lot of very delicate, nuanced conversations around the human impact of automation and AI, and it got into the philosophical and ethical."

More and more, Ross was invited to take part in these conversations. Others would ask, "Well, what do you think of this Lorna – ethically?" She realized that they were transposing design, because it is people-centered, to be the gatekeeper for ethics too.

Ross struggled with this and decided to create an internal team called the Human Insights Lab. She reached out to a friend who was a professor of humanities at Trinity College, Dublin. Ross partnered with her and her department. "We had access to historians, philosophers, ethicists," she said. "I told people inside the company, 'If you want me to be the gatekeeper for these ethical issues, then I'm going to be pulling in subject-matter experts in this area.'" This design-led team would add the expertise, both philosophically or ethically, to handle these very delicate conversations.

As an idea – at least a theoretical one – her plan was well received, at first. "We ran workshops with the analytics guys, and we were talking about ethical implications, and the idea of thinking more philosophically and ethically about technology." As the discussions continued, however, the participants became more nervous: "They thought, 'We're not accountable for understanding the ethical, social, and political implications of what we developed. It's not what we do.'"

The response from her Accenture colleagues was, "Well, it's fine, but we don't really want to unpack those conversations anyway, so let's just have some response for clients that is kind of high-level, in terms of the implications to humans, and if you can reassure them everything's going to be okay, then that's good enough."

"It's a bit like asking someone who designs a switch that ends up on a bomb," she said. "Are they accountable for the people that the bomb killed?" The technologists were abstracted from ethical implications, or accountability. "So we kept thinking, 'Where is accountability in these conversations?' and it was a can that kept getting kicked down the road, and no one really owned it … It made people really, really, really uncomfortable."

The team was asked to turn it into less of a critique, less of a nuanced understanding about the complexity of ethical topics, and more about looking for opportunities where the consultancy's clients could understand how they could effectively use design insights to manipulate people.

Ross paused and laughed at this. "So, we were an insight group, and we were trying to use insights to be a kind of cautionary or critique, and people said, 'Well, we'd prefer if the insights were ones that could be turned into a financial advantage.'"

Ross ended up leaving, largely because she understood that her intent to broaden the narrative around emerging tech and the role of design had been stymied. She had wanted to show how design could be a bridge to pull other expertise or opinions in, and that it could be a conduit to being more inclusive. But the whole intent had been turned on its head. "The lab actually ended up within a marketing group, where they started to explore nudge theory, and more, around, 'How do we understand human motivation and how behavior is shaped, and how can we use that to our advantage?'"

The discomfort Ross described is shared by many designers, who feel that their work is judged on a single metric: whether it helps the (financial) bottom line. The experience is symptomatic of a reductionist mental model in organizations: Only the numbers matter, and the most important numbers are financial. This model is founded on a set of assumptions that have serious consequences for design, and for society.

The Epistemology Bind

We discussed the use of fictitious and inappropriate numbers in service of the extractive business model in chapter 5. More broadly, many designers report that design is not taken seriously in their organizations because it runs up against accepted ways of knowing. Underlying the resistance to design are hidden assumptions about what constitutes truth, and the dominant logic of finance.

How the Epistemology Bind Is Experienced

The Epistemology bind arises from hidden assumptions that are always there, but rarely acknowledged. But designers feel its impact every day, primarily in the ways qualitative research is discounted or disdained, and in the pervasive bias for the bottom line. They are asked to understand and create, and then the understanding they produce is considered inferior to other forms of knowledge.

Qualitative Research Seen as Illegitimate

Designers experience the Epistemology bind when quantitative data is elevated in importance above other ways of knowing.

The foundation of design is insight, and this insight is found in the stories users tell. Designers conduct research that explores these stories, to understand users and their context. Necessarily, this research is qualitative, based on in-depth, unstructured interviews with small numbers of participants and in-context observation.

Many managers, however, do not hold this kind of research in high regard. Commonly, they will criticize this research on the basis of small samples. As we will discuss below, this criticism shows a profound misunderstanding of the different purposes of quantitative and qualitative research. Yet at the same time, organizations place heavy reliance on picking winning ideas through focus groups, which not only rely on small numbers, but are notoriously subject to biases due to dominant individuals and the reluctance of respondents to share private information.

In design, the Epistemology bind becomes visible when designers are forced to use numbers and finance as their primary source of truth.

In Oslo, the Norwegian capital, hospitals were amalgamating multiple locations across the municipality into a centralized office tower.

Teams of doctors and administrators scrambled to develop a plan on how each specialty would best utilize its space. "They had two months to hold meetings, and they were given past figures on patient volumes, some future projections, and the square footage of their floor in the new building," Josina Vink, author of the iceberg model we discussed in chapter 6, told us.

"[B]ut what they had was completely inadequate to make decisions," they went on. "You can point to the numbers and say, 'Well, that's how I made an evidence-based decision,' but that's meaningless. In reality, most of the work making big decisions is extremely intuitive. People don't like to admit it, but you need to use your instincts, which rely on years and years of experience."

Narratives and lived experience were discounted by management, who saw numbers as reliable and unbiased. In this way of thinking, "truth" relies on quantification.

Yet in business and government, quantitative research is the lingua franca. "What gets measured, gets managed" is a common maxim; and when what gets measured are numbers – particularly those driving efficiency and profit – people tend to discount, or dismiss, other kinds of information. In doing so, they overlook the critical input that is the cornerstones of good design: understanding others and their context, and creative instincts that come from practicing a craft.

Bottom Line Bias

Organizations are dominated by a financialized epistemology. Many people working within organizations are unaware of how the hidden assumption of superiority of financial information shapes their attitudes and actions.

Designers understand the need for businesses to be profitable. But design practice focuses on understanding non-financial considerations as well. The discourse in many organizations, public and private, though, is entirely about finance. Designers are hired with job postings that promise to improve people's lives, transform systems, and innovate industries. Meanwhile, they are constantly confronted with demands to justify their ideas based on short-term profitability *alone*, rather than other criteria such as value to users, society, or the planet.

Even within the publicly funded Canadian healthcare system, where ostensibly patient welfare matters most, the invisible force of financialized epistemology can stifle patient-centric design. At UHN in Toronto, Mike Lovas works on improving the experience of patients undergoing cancer treatment. While the hospital is well aware of its poor results in this area and the need to improve patient experience, the focus is on financialization.

"People devalue patient experience," said Lovas. "It's not sexy. It's not easy to publish. People who invest in innovation – the boards, the foundations, the donors, scientists, and granting agencies who fund the science – they all want the next big blockbuster. They want to find a breakthrough that will make hundreds of millions of dollars."

Researchers studying the rapid rise of funding for medical initiatives, technology, and programs have also criticized the ability of these technologies to achieve adequate patient outcomes if the initiatives are financially motivated.[1] In one 2019 paper, Bennett Holman, assistant professor of history and philosophy of science at Yonsei University, South Korea, argued that "[Medicine] must also account for the fact that industry influences which questions get asked and which methods are chosen to answer them ... that many experiments are conducted as marketing exercises (e.g., seeding trials)."[2]

Even in so-called purpose-driven organizations, the bottom line is often the only thing that matters. "Leadership says they want to make life better for our clients, but then they are addicted to using McKinsey," said a design leader in such an organization, who wished to remain anonymous. "They want the kind of data they can show the board of directors, so the financial metrics take over."

Yet when designers challenge the prevailing paradigm, they are regularly dismissed or silenced. Eloise Smith-Foster is a lead designer at a Nordic design studio, Futurice. Like many designers, Smith-Foster believes that design skills are critical to finding a way out of our current problems. On the day of our interview, these problems could not have been more obvious, as smoke filled the skies of North America, the result of unprecedented Canadian wildfires caused by climate change. In New York City, people were experiencing the worst air quality rating in the world.[3]

"It's difficult to broaden the scope to include social issues," argued Smith-Foster. "If issues about oppression in the supply chain ... or biodiversity loss come up, they get shut down by key power holders."

"There's this constant sense of urgency that shuts down different points of view," she continued. "They don't want to reflect ... they want to see designers bring quick wins and silver bullets." Quick wins, of course, meaning quick financial wins.

The Epistemology bind arises when designers' findings are discounted because of their lack of connection to the evidence required within financialized organizations. "Often we will find some unmet needs that would really improve our client's financial well-being," said a designer working within a major bank, who wished to remain unnamed. "But immediately we are asked to show how it will make more money ... and the idea gets twisted into something that can be used to manipulate the people it was meant to help."

In spite of these concerns, designers all too often capitulate to financialized epistemology by adopting the dominant logic, turning the intuitive design process into a predictable assembly line with numeric outputs.

"[Design] is utilized in linear, reductive ways, to instrumentalize and to proceduralize design, and turn it into a series of repeatable steps," said Dr. Matt Ratto, associate professor and associate dean of research at the University of Toronto's Faculty of Information, and founder of multiple technology startups. "Ultimately, this reduces it to an 'automatable,' trackable, metricable phenomenon. This ... can help designers represent and explain their value-add to an organization – but this runs the risk of helping deskill and devalue the practice."

Some try to straddle the epistemologies of business and design. Labels like "business design," "integrative thinking," and even design thinking itself attempt to combine design and business methods, but usually with an instrumental view of design, as another way for a business to attain superior financial results. Such attempts to merge design and business ignore the much larger – non-financial – value design can create and the trade-offs necessary to realize it.

Understanding the Epistemology Bind

Underlying the experience of the Epistemology bind are a set of assumptions about truth, objectivity, and purpose. These mostly go unacknowledged but nonetheless have a very real impact. The assumptions arise from the legacy of colonialism, the illusion of objectivity, and financialization.

The Legacy of Colonialism

Organizations tend to prioritize quantitative research over qualitative. This is rooted in the history of colonization and in assumptions about social stratification.

Designers regularly spend time with 'users,' applying qualitative approaches such as open-ended interviewing, in-situ observations, co-designing, and iterating as their way of knowing if something is true. Historically, these methods grew out of anthropology and sociology, which sought new ways to understand people and society. Like today's designers, anthropology pioneers Frank Boas and Margaret

Mead found themselves rebelling against the dominant epistemology, which used numbers to categorize people and the world.

In their time, science and numbers were used to demonstrate the superiority of the white male. According to anthropology historian Charles King, "A little over a century ago, any educated person knew that the world worked in certain obvious ways. Each [human] was fated to be more or less intelligent, idle, rule bound, or warlike. Politics properly belonged to men ... Immigrants tended to dilute national vigor. Animals deserved kindness, and backwards peoples, a few rungs above animals, were owed our help, but not our respect. The poor were poor because of their own inadequacies. Nature favored the robust colonizer over the benighted native. People were neatly packaged into cultures from 'primitive' to 'advanced.' The idea of a natural ranking of human types shaped everything. The allure of quantification was irresistible."[4]

Indigenous ways of knowing, subsistence farming methods that had flourished for millennia, and the position of women within matriarchal societies were largely ignored in favor of systems that could be quantified and managed using Western capitalist logic. Today, Western management also assigns people to types and categories – such as market segments.[5]

Cognitive imperialism still discredits other knowledge systems and values.[6] Science scholar Vandana Shiva describes the notion of science and capitalism as universal truth as the "Monoculture of the Mind." Shiva argues that the use of the prefix "scientific" for the modern systems, and "unscientific" for traditional knowledge systems has less to do with knowledge and more to do with power.[7]

Dr. François Bastien at the Gustavson School of Management in Victoria, British Columbia is an assistant professor and the academic director of the MBA in Advancing Reconciliation. "In management schools," argued Bastien, "we have to move away from cognitive imperialism, this idea that there is one way of seeing the world: The Western way of seeing the world is the standard, and everything else is inferior."

Bastien compared today's business missionaries with the Christian missionaries of past centuries. "In the beginning, it was, 'How can we save Indigenous communities with Christianity? Let's send missionaries and Bibles.' Well, capitalism has replaced Christianity. And now it's, 'How can we save Indigenous communities with entrepreneurship and capitalism?' And we're sending business educators and marketing textbooks."

Biases arising from past worldviews are being questioned as never before. Along with transparency and accountability, consumers, employees, and society now expect organizations to be willing to grapple with systemic racism and sexism, environmental collapse, and income inequality. Because their job is to pay close attention to the wider world outside the organization, designers are more attuned to these shifts than most within the organizations they work for.

FRANÇOIS BASTIEN, PHD, PETER B. GUSTAVSON SCHOOL OF BUSINESS, UNIVERSITY OF VICTORIA

François (Frank) Bastien is an assistant professor at the Peter B. Gustavson School of Business at the University of Victoria. As a Huron-Wendat from the Indigenous community of Wendake, he has observed incongruities between Indigenous ways of organizing and contemporary colonial models. He aims to translate Indigenous knowledge and challenge colonial assumptions.

When he began his studies at a business school, he was struck by the contrast between the Indigenous ways of thinking he was used to and the Western colonial approach. "If you look at the seventh generation principle ... we make a decision based on how it affects seven generations – much different than, well, when I die, I'm not here anymore, and I only live here 80 years. For me, it was a stark contrast to what I was certainly used to."

He is critical of "Western ways of seeing the world as a standard, and everything [else] is inferior." But, he says, "With Western ways of knowing and thinking, we might be at a point of saturation, and to find solutions to these wicked problems, we're gonna have to get out of that world."

He is also critical of token efforts by businesses and universities to indigenize. "We put the responsibility on you [Indigenous people] now to show us the light. We're not going to do any work ... we're going to put a whole bunch of territorial acknowledgments on our email signatures."

"Indigenization is not about equal opportunity ... [or] about counts of Indigenous faculty members. It's not about how many tepees you have on campus, [or] how much space you have for Indigenous students. Indigenization is about a paradigm shift in thinking."

Though he had mixed feelings about becoming a business professor, Bastien believes that it is critical to educate future leaders so we do not perpetuate the old paradigm. "Business schools attract 19% of undergraduate students. So if we don't do it, if we don't indigenize and decolonize, these are people that become leaders in organization, they're just going to perpetuate what they learn here. So in order to change things, even though it's very incommensurable with my way of seeing the world, I thought that that was the best platform to do my work."

Positivism and the Illusion of Objectivity

The idea of "objectivity" is an illusion. Designers, because they work directly with a variety of stakeholders like users and frontline staff, are extremely familiar with seeing different worldviews of the same product or service. In one landmark study, about 85 per cent of participants indicated that they were more objective than the average member of the group from which they were drawn – a statistical impossibility.[8]

This illusion draws upon a positivist understanding of the world and leads designers to become alienated from the organizations they seek to support. The positivist philosophy holds that every rationally justifiable assertion can be scientifically verified or is capable of logical or mathematical proof; in particular, numbers provide a sharp distinction between facts and subjectivity.

As we have seen, management, quantitative data, and financial metrics are the products of a specific culture and social system, in which numbers are considered the only "truth." Spreadsheets, KPI dashboards, and quantitative metrics are the primary means of understanding and decision making in organizations. "When I started at BCG Digital Ventures, we spent a couple of weeks learning how to prove something is true," said design strategist Jayesh Srivistava. "We learned how to make models and forecasts, and it was fascinating to see what was considered most important to convince business leaders to make a decision."

Even the so-called gold standard of scientific objectivity, randomized control trials (RCTs), have well-known sources of systematic bias. Dr. Emily Freeman is a social scientist who began her career at Bridgeable as a design researcher. She now works inside one of the world's largest pharmaceutical companies in a new role focused on patient-focused drug development.

"Everything we know about clinical trials was standardized against the white male body. Everything." she told us. "It wasn't until 1993 that women were *allowed* in clinical trials in the United States. I mean, think about it, 1993. That's not that long ago! Our treatments were always standardized against the white male body. And everything fell from that: biomarkers, treatments, clinical guidelines."

Yet the scientific method is seen as producing truth so universal that it transcends cultural and religious knowledge: Math, for example, is referred to as a "universal language." The supposed superiority of these methods means that, for many managers, the only way to know something is true is to represent it with numbers.

Conversely, if there are no numbers, a finding cannot be accepted as true. While designers use a variety of research methods, they rely primarily on qualitative research and co-creative practices to know if something is true. But design and management sources of truth have different goals, different requirements, and different epistemological underpinnings.

For designers, the purpose of qualitative research is to uncover insights, not to seek statistical validation – that's the job of quantitative research. Yet it is no less rigorous than quantitative research.

Rigor is established in different ways from quantitative research. Contrary to popular belief, sample sizes do not indicate validity and are usually much smaller in ethnographic studies than the norms for quantitative research. Rigor is established through *triangulation* (using multiple methods to arrive at themes and hypotheses), *representation* (ensuring that all important segments are adequately represented in the sample), and *thematic saturation* (themes start to repeat themselves).

Designers also make things in order to think. They engage in prototyping and iteration to solve problems, relying on experience and intuition to know when something will work. The craft of design is often underestimated because it does not lend itself well to the dominant form of proof, objective quantification. How do you quantify Apple's seamless hardware-software integration, or how much a family loved a vacation experience? Often the most important things are the hardest to measure.

As Jony Ive, arguably the most commercially successful designer of a generation, argues "[Inside companies] it's much easier to talk about something that you can measure with a number. There is a dangerous assumption that we're having these conversations because they're the only important ones. Because you can't assign a system of numbers to make the relative judgments that need to be made."[9]

All forms of research, including co-creation, qualitative research, surveys, and statistical models, are subject to human judgment. They each have different purposes, yet, within organizations, numbers are treated as superior because of the illusion of objectivity.

Financialization

Rooted in positivism, finance and accounting tools dominate organizational discourse. By emphasizing accounting measures to the exclusion of everything else, organizations claim a reliable and universal form of knowledge. Yet these tools exclude a great deal of what is valuable, and that benefits certain groups over others.

It has been argued that the financialization of corporate decision-making has been the prime source of inequity and instability in economic performance over the past three decades.[10] Unsustainable exploitation and grievous acts of inhumanity have been attributed to accounting's ability to mask the humanity of those it commodified.[11,12] The era of financialization has been marked by an enormous increase in the size of the financial sector and significantly changed income distribution in favor of those who have capital.[13] Just as colonial powers discounted local ways of knowing and values to exploit resources and labor, the financialized epistemology masks the inhumanity of organizational actions.

Some economists question the conventional assumptions about what we value in Western capitalist societies. According to Mariana Mazzucato, Professor in the Economics of Innovation and Public Value at University College London, financialization has made us believe that market price is the only thing we should value. In her 2018 book, *The Value of Everything: Making and Taking in the Global Economy*, Mazzucato argues that economic theory has failed to clearly delineate the difference between value creation and value extraction.[14]

A financialized epistemology places value only on those things that have a price, failing to recognize the morally, socially, and politically dubious consequences of the actions of corporations and governments. In a 2014 paper co-authored with Alan Shipman of the Open University, Mazucatto argues that conventionally measured GDP – the primary benchmark by which economic performance is measured – understates, or completely omits, factors like quality unless it is reflected in price; innovation that *reduces* prices; innovation that increases quality of life, such as investments in environmental sustainability, R&D, artistic endeavors, and many others.

Mazzucato has an alternative. Rather than focus on numbers, she believes we should be unleashing our creativity on bold challenges – moonshots – to drive long-term value. "Innovation and the commercialization of ideas do not happen because you want them to: They happen along the way to solving bigger problems," she writes.[15]

Canadian prime minister and former central bank governor Mark Carney also believes that we have become focussed on price and not value, comparing Amazon's trillion-dollar market capitalization with the low value placed on the Amazon rainforest.[16]

In an attempt to mitigate their effects on the planet and society, some organizations are adopting Environmental and Social Governance (ESG) initiatives. Many of these are well intended, but conventional measures do not reflect their value. While progress has been made with measurement systems for ESG investing, they have been criticized for their ineffectiveness in driving environmental and social value[17] and have been largely ineffective in changing corporate behavior.[18] ESG has been plagued by issues related to finding a suitable approach to ratings and data.[19],[20]

Designers worry about how financialization frames the discourse around environmental and social value. As Dan Hill, director of the School of Design at the University of Melbourne, told us, "These can sometimes be called social or environmental capital, although I think that's another example of financialization creeping in where society and the environment are seen the same as financial capital – like they exist in bank accounts."

Hill goes on to explain how unconsciously applying the epistemic premise of financialization stymies our ability to solve problems. "The issue of financialization is that it has pervaded through our culture to such a degree that it feels like it must have always been there. It's the way that we do things, it always works. You can just look at the climate to say, we clearly have a massive issue on our hands. As we manage that transition, the issue on the table is that we haven't accepted that financialization has precipitated it. And so we're trying to financialize our way out of the mess that created it."

The need to see everything through a financial lens stifles designers' ability to unlock new forms of value that are not measurable by conventional means, but will make our organizations more resilient.

Loosening the Epistemology Bind

Challenging the Epistemology bind is uncomfortable, because it exposes things many would prefer to ignore: the underlying weaknesses in our ways of knowing, the exploitative role played by businesses and governments, and the disturbing assumptions that underlie the ways we measure things. Designers have dealt with these issues in a variety of ways: by being clear and intentional about the work they undertake, by reaching out to a community of like-minded people, and by taking steps to understand power dynamics.

Choose Work Intentionally

Designers need to be intentional about the work they choose.

As head of innovation at Digitas, Lizzie Shupak designed digital experiences for some of the world's largest companies. "For me, at the heart of design is intention. What design brings is intentional thought, directing attention and resources to create something," said Shupak from her home in London.

In 2017, Shupak decided to leave agency life to co-found a studio with a focus on regenerative business, and helping organizations make sustainable and equitable choices that benefit not just shareholders but the wider world. To meet this ambitious goal, she found that clearly stating the team's intentions helped combat the financialized epistemology. "When we started, my partner and I agreed that we wanted to work with globally recognized brands, and we wanted to be able to be ourselves, and not have to try to pretend to be someone else to try and fit in."

To keep their intent in focus, Shupak's team crystallized their values into statements that they use every day in their work. "By being very up front about our values, they act as a filter for who we work with. It's important for me to live intentionally from my own values because I am a woman and the mother of two girls. There's something in the primal, emotional, intuitive, which is seen as feminine. And historically that's not a way of knowing that's seen as reasonable. Somehow, we've put these really narrow parameters around what's acceptable and what's legitimate." Explicitly defining their own values and committing to showing up in a way that was authentic allowed the team to challenge the dominant epistemology.

Similarly, husband-and-wife design team George Aye and Sara Cantor created Greater Good Studio out of a desire to align their work and their values. At first, they would judge how well a project aligned with their values on a case-by-case basis. But as they scaled, they needed to find a consistent way to evaluate their clients and projects. In order to deal with this, they came up with a system they affectionately call "Gut Check." Rather than deciding on each project individually, they identified a series of questions based on their values and experiences on what matters to them most. The list has now expanded to

50 questions and is a living document that continues to evolve over time.

Intentionally aligning project selection with your values is an ongoing job that requires meaningful time and energy. Cantor knows her team has chosen the harder road and expects the work to be difficult. In an interview, she said, "Part of being a designer is just not being deterred and essentially thinking around barriers, because everything is hard. I mean, what change that's worthwhile is easy?"

Find Your People

Challenging the dominant epistemology within an organization can be a lonely road. Many designers look to groups both inside and outside of their organizations for support.

Outside of work at Futurice, Eloise Smith-Foster runs an activist organization, Design Activists for Regenerative Futures. She argues that engaging in a community of like-minded people outside work helps manage the tensions and tradeoffs within the organization. "I work within the business epistemology, trying to make change within it. Then I'm also working outside as an activist," she says. People are drawn to the group because of the peer support it offers.

"Designers in the group are wanting to make change, but finding it extremely slow within their organization, and so they feel frustrated. By coming together we can offer inspiration and peer support." Among other topics, the group tackles issues around what activism looks like within a company setting. These run the gamut from drastic steps like going on strike to consistently challenging the status quo: "gentle, quiet activism, which is changing your interpersonal relationships, and then how you relate within the business."

ELOISE SMITH-FOSTER:
DESIGN ACTIVISTS FOR A REGENERATIVE FUTURE

Eloise Smith-Foster is a designer working for a Nordic design studio at their UK branch. By day, her work focuses on large-scale service and UX design projects. Smith-Foster also founded Design Activists for a Regenerative Future, an international group of designers working collectively to advance social and environmental issues.

"I started Design Activists for a Regenerative Future because other designers and I felt the pace of change inside our organizations was far too slow. Finding people who have a different view, knowing you're not alone, and who also feel that things could be different helps me a lot. That collectivism brings me solace.

"I think about my principles and values a lot. One value is co-liberation: working together for a just and equitable world for people and the planet. No one is free until we are all free. And within that, I'm always trying to analyze and look out for colonial patterns like white saviorism.

"Our organizations are rooted in colonialism and white supremacy. I don't want to fall into the trap of thinking 'we need to help these people.' Designers can be very egotistical and believe they can save the world and are doing the right thing. We must always start with humility and curiosity, and recognize [that] other people's, including managers', points of view are equally valid. They need to be understood, whether you agree with them or not.

"Designers must develop the skill of dealing with conflict to challenge existing conditions. It's a white supremacist cultural pattern to avoid conflict and difference. Expanding the scope to ecology and social issues will make things more difficult. Business will have to reconsider their place deeply. Challenges can be shut down because they're undermining the business paradigm.

"There's an underlying belief that the future will continue on the same as the present. But we know that is never the case. When I'm having some doubts I think, once one woman said to another, 'we should have the vote.' And you know they were told, 'You're so naïve. You're crazy. That's never gonna happen.' So, what's the parallel today? Designers must be ready for conflict because these conversations threaten people's position and power."

Understand Power Dynamics

Many designers are unprepared for power dynamics and often don't understand how decisions are made within their organization.

Mapping can be a powerful tool for understanding how things actually work. "Often when we run training, we get designers to map out stakeholder relationships. Who do you actually need to bring on board? Who do you need to influence? Who's actually setting the brief? Who's influencing your client?" said Sarah Drummond, director of the School of Good Services.

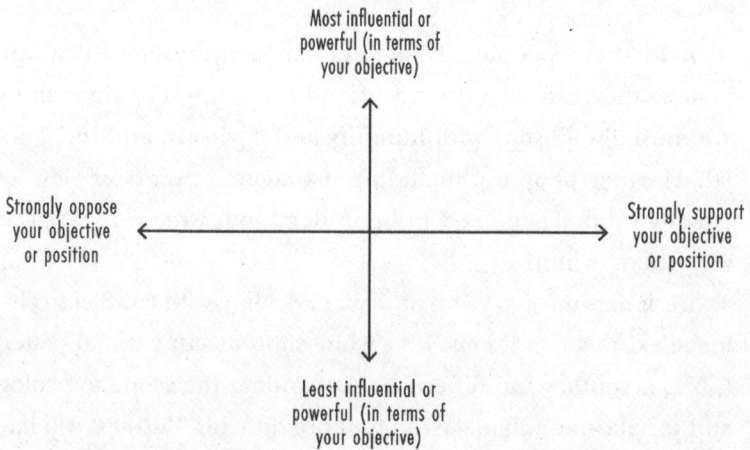

Figure 7.1 *Power mapping.*
(https://beautifultrouble.org/toolbox/tool/power-mapping/)

Smith-Foster is also experimenting with different stakeholder mapping techniques early on in projects to understand how decisions are made. "Something I'd like to do more earlier on in projects is apply tools from systems change around power mapping and value-flow mapping. It's valuable to understand those problematic patterns or dynamics to the surface early. Knowing how power works supports conversations about project tensions later on."

One method that might be helpful is power mapping, a tool used by social activists to describe power relations. An example, from the toolbox of activist training group Beautiful Trouble, is shown in Figure 7.1. The map classifies stakeholders according to their degree of influence on the decision maker, and their extent of agreement with the proposal.

In a discussion paper for the International Food Policy Research Institute,[21] Eva Schiffer described how power mapping was effectively applied to analyze the governance effects of community-based natural resource management in Namibia. The actors were depicted as board-game figures on "range-of-action cards" and placed on "power towers" to represent their level of power. The method produced a three-dimensional sketch that both provided quantitative data and guided qualitative discussion about the power of different actors, its underpinnings and its effects.

We have left the discussion of the Epistemology bind last, because it is in many ways the most difficult to address. Dealing with it demands not only deep self-examination, but confronting powerful people with no interest in confronting colonialism, white privilege, and the many social ills that arise from our exploitative history. But the potential – for enlightened businesses, for governments, for society, *and* for designers – is there. The world needs the unique perspective of designers to navigate a path forward that is more just, and more conscious, than the one we have taken so far.

◻

8 Value, Redesigned

Throughout this book, we have showcased the double binds that commonly get in the way of designers and managers creating new forms of value. We have seen how the business world's embrace of design has expanded design's profile, and at the same time how the unconscious biases of business, from workstyle to risk attitudes, have limited its true potential. Encouragingly, however, we have also seen how designers are learning to deal with the challenges, as organizations deliver the kind of impact designers believe is possible, and managers say they want.

As corporate hype settles down, a more nuanced view of design is emerging, and along with it, new possibilities for design. The frustration of many designers lies in the gap between the promise of helping users, improving products and services, and transforming society, versus the pressure to be a limitless engine of corporate growth. By understanding and untying the binds, designers and managers can collaborate to deliver solutions to the economic, ethical, social, and environmental concerns that plague our society.

In this final chapter, we take a broader look at the role design can play in building a better future. We disagree with those who think design is a fad whose time has come and gone – on the contrary, we see great potential for designers and managers to work together.

Design Is Maturing, Not Dying

Over a dozen years ago, Bruce Nussbaum famously wrote design thinking's epitaph.[1] Since then, it has been likened to everything from syphilis to bullshit.[2] Yet, to paraphrase Mark Twain, reports of design's death are greatly exaggerated. On the contrary, design is maturing – and, like a caterpillar transformed into a butterfly, its mature state will differ significantly from its previous incarnations.

A More Sophisticated Understanding of Design

We met John Pipino, or Pip, project lead at Doblin, in chapter 2. A designer and professor of design for over 30 years, he has seen design trends come and go. Pip believes that what's happening to design is similar to other elements of business life. "It's not unique to design," he says, but a recognizable pattern: Initially, ideas are compartmentalized but ultimately break free and wind up diffused throughout business.

"Technology's a really accessible parallel," he goes on. "There was a time that only specialists used computers, and they were in concentrated areas, even concentrated rooms, with special fire-suppressant systems. And gradually, over time – it took a generation – it became understood that everyone in business would use a keyboard." In the same way, design has jumped out of its compartment and become common knowledge.

In the 1990s, Gartner, a research firm, defined the "Technology Hype Cycle." The THC described a human dimension of tech hype that seemed all too familiar. Its basic structure was like a roller coaster: After an initial period of *positive hype*, fueled by media and the self-interest of a technology's promoters, a technology's visibility would peak and go into freefall (*negative hype*) until it bottomed out. In time, it would partly recover from this and settle at a plateau of mainstream adoption, where the real-world benefits of the technology were demonstrated and accepted.

Design has – thankfully – left positive hype behind and passed through the trough of disillusionment represented by Nussbaum and others. Businesses now largely understand design and recognize the challenges involved in implementing it in a corporate setting. This has led some, such as Procter & Gamble and Johnson & Johnson, to abandon design as "the next big thing," or reduce its influence as an independent entity. Meanwhile, many designers, faced with the extractive mindset of the large organizations they work for, are abandoning the outmoded corporate framing of design, and are applying their skills under titles that don't even contain the word "design."

Yet after decades of weekend workshops, Design 101s, executive courses, and MBA design specializations, a generation of managers is quite familiar with user research, prototyping, and iterating. Perhaps more importantly, this generation has established pluralistic ways of bringing in different viewpoints and challenging entrenched "insider" perspectives. These changes do not indicate the demise of design; on the contrary, they bear witness to its wide acceptance and its assimilation into day-to-day business, rather than being treated as a separate entity. Not *everyone* can be a designer – as previously argued by some management gurus – but managers understand design more clearly than ever before.

Design is at an exciting time in its life cycle because the baseline of design in private- and public-sector organizations is now higher than ever. Designers are taking steps to ensure they are the makers, not takers, of value.

Designers are moving on from flashy corporate roles to organizations where they can apply their skills without the hype. "We'd been so influenced by business metrics that what I did was barely design anymore. [My] new role isn't even called design, but I get to work on something I see is important" said one senior designer who had recently left a role inside a major bank.

Designers are becoming more reflective about how design is being practiced. "At [major technology consulting firm], they have completely lost touch with what it means to do good design work … they're just checking a box to sell technology projects," lamented a senior executive who had worked closely with designers throughout their career. "It took some work, but I've replaced them with a couple of small design firms." Even those inside global accounting firms that once devoured design studios as part of their expansion ambitions are seeing the consequences of the double binds. "Deloitte, where good companies go to die" was the characterization of one senior leader who had witnessed multiple studios fail under their financialized logic.

But the ability to create value depends on how design is practiced. Designers can bring a degree of sophistication to design practice that far surpasses routine user personas and journey maps. It takes years of experience to recognize patterns in qualitative data, to synthesize as well as analyze, to craft thoughtful products and services, and to understand how to navigate the complexities required to implement them. As design becomes more ubiquitous, organizations will develop a more nuanced understanding of how their competitiveness relies on richer applications of design, and the underlying logics that empower it.

To help bring this about, designers will need to pay attention to the "plumbing" of innovation – the underlying infrastructure that facilitates design work. We saw earlier how designers are often denied access to end users and stakeholders; how collaborative work across functions can be impeded by organizational structures; and how stage-gate systems can shut down promising ideas too early. By working with their organizations to remove such structural obstacles and establish systems that favor creative and contextually informed work, designers can enrich design work and safeguard its integrity.

A New Role for Design

In chapter 1, we saw that attitudes in the business community are shifting away from an extractive mindset emphasizing share-holder returns above all other considerations, to one embracing a broader range of stakeholders, communities, and the planet. Throughout this book, we have noted how considerations of ethics, diversity, decolonization, transparency, and accountability increasingly influence strategic decision-making. In spite of the recent rightward shift in US politics, we consider this a fundamental mindset change. We expect the trend to continue, and even accelerate, in decades to come.

As organizations become ever more aligned with societal needs, designers are well-positioned to help the transition into a different economy, one that reflects values of social justice and environmental awareness. Because they – uniquely – bridge their organization's internal environment with perspectives from the wider world, they can expand their scope further still, and embrace pressing social and environmental problems. They have access to the mindset, and the skills, to understand and redesign the underlying systemic barriers, beliefs, and assumptions that threaten our collective future.

The transformative potential of design rests on its ability to enable people to move, intentionally, beyond shaping materials like new technologies and products to underlying social structures.[3]

New Problems, New Potential

As technology advances, designers are already tackling emerging problems in new ways based on their newfound position and authority. At the same time, design itself is changing as new movements arise to help tackle massive problems.

Preparing for/Adapting to the 4IR

The Fourth Industrial Revolution (4IR) is upon us, and designers have an important role to play. Four technology categories that are driving the 4IR:[4]

1. *Connectivity, data, and computational power:* cloud technology, the Internet, blockchain, sensors
2. *Analytics and intelligence:* advanced analytics, machine learning, artificial intelligence
3. *Human–machine interaction:* virtual reality (VR) and augmented reality (AR), robotics and automation, autonomous guided vehicles
4. *Advanced engineering:* additive manufacturing (such as 3-D printing), renewable energy, nanoparticles

Technology is bringing about the 4IR – yet it would be a mistake to conclude that the 4IR is just about technology. It creates new demands on executives to think strategically and make sense of ambiguous information as never before.

A CEO of a manufacturer of small aircraft told us that the things that kept him awake at night were two changes that would transform his industry: additive manufacturing (3-D printing), and electric aircraft. To deal with these challenges, he needed even junior managers to think strategically, not just operationally: "I need people who can get their head out of the weeds," he said.

But the advance of technology is not just a business problem. According to the World Economic Forum, it is a *new chapter in human development*:

> The speed, breadth and depth of this revolution is forcing us to rethink how countries develop, how organizations create value and even what it means to be human. The Fourth Industrial Revolution is about more than just technology-driven change; it is an opportunity to help everyone, including leaders, policy-makers and people from all income groups and nations, to harness converging technologies in order to create an inclusive, human-centered future. The real opportunity is to look beyond technology, and find ways to give the greatest number of people the ability to positively impact their families, organizations, and communities.[5]

Many designers we spoke to expressed regret for their complicity in the destructive social impacts during the rise of app and web development. They are taking a more proactive stance with AI.

Robert Fabricant, co-founder of Dalberg Design and a former VP of creative at the global creative consultancy Frog Design, commented on the challenges to user advocacy in the development of new AI technologies: In a 2024 post, he wrote of his concern "with the broader question of advocacy as it relates to ... the rise of GenAI capabilities that have the potential to cut 'users' completely out of the equation."[6]

While Lorna Ross struggled to have design play a role in applying ethics to technology (chapter 7), Fabricant argues that designers must help bring in the perspective of people impacted by emergent technologies to ensure they positively impact the world. He points to the limits of past efforts: "Research reports will only get you so far. And legal / compliance risks are generally seen as afterthoughts," he writes.

Technology poses further challenges, beyond the tendency to cut out users. Mariana Mazzucato, whom we met in chapter 7, argues that the tech industry has a massive impact on the planet while diverting resources from critical areas such as housing – and AI's impact is among the worst. "Large language models such as ChatGPT," she writes, "are some of the most energy-guzzling technologies of all."[7] Google's global data center and Meta's ambitious plans for a new AI research supercluster raise further concerns that AI's energy impact will increase. Other technologies, such as lithium mining, are associated with pollution and human rights violations.

Mazzucato argues for governments to take action: "In an era where we expect businesses to do more than just make profits for their shareholders, governments need to evaluate the organizations they fund and partner with, based on whether their actions will result in concrete successes for people and the planet."

Changes to government policy and funding will certainly play a role in tempering the tendency of some businesses to move fast, break things, and leave others to worry about the consequences. But there is a role for designers too: to push their organizations to think more broadly about the systemic, societal, and environmental impact of technology.

To do so, they need to broaden their own thinking. Two examples of how this change in thinking can be brought about – transition design and capital design – follow.

Transition Design

Design's ability to make sense of the complex and ambiguous makes it attractive to executives who deal with difficult business problems – such as talent management, product and service innovation, and application of technology – on a daily basis. Yet these problems occur within a wider context. Talent management, for example, is influenced by employee expectations, which in turn are influenced by factors such as technology, the gig economy, social movements, employees' expectations around corporate behavior, and many others.

Traditional design approaches, argues design professor Terry Irwin, situate problems within relatively narrow socio-temporal contexts. To tackle problems at the level of social and environmental systems, designers are now talking about transition design.

According to Irwin, transition design brings systems thinking to a higher level, by visualizing and mapping complex problems and their interconnections and interdependencies, using methods such as giga-mapping; situating them within large, spatio-temporal contexts; identifying and bridging stakeholder needs and interests; helping stakeholders co-visualize desirable futures; and identifying leverage points in the larger system.

As shown in Figure 8.1, transition design is a perspective rather than a fixed process, bringing together compelling visions of the future, new ways of designing, an open, mindful, reflective, and collaborative mindset, and theories of change within the natural and social worlds.

If designers and organizations are to work together to redesign value, their task is much bigger than just understanding the "next big thing," what frivolous product or service users want: They need to pay attention to relationships between businesses, governments,

Co-created, long-term
visions of sustainable
futures

Visions evolve as
a result of new
ways of designing

VISIONS FOR
TRANSITION

Visions informed
by biological and
social systems

ystems interventions
offer long-term
solutions

NEW WAYS
OF DESIGNING

TRANSITION
DESIGN
FRAMEWORK

THEORIES
OF CHANGE

Deep understanding
of change, based
on theories
from diverse fields

Posture and mindset
changes give rise to new
design approaches

POSTURE
& MINDSET

Understanding shapes
mindsets, and creates thirst
for new knowledge

Mindfulness, humility,
collaboration, reflectiveness,
optimism, openness, respect

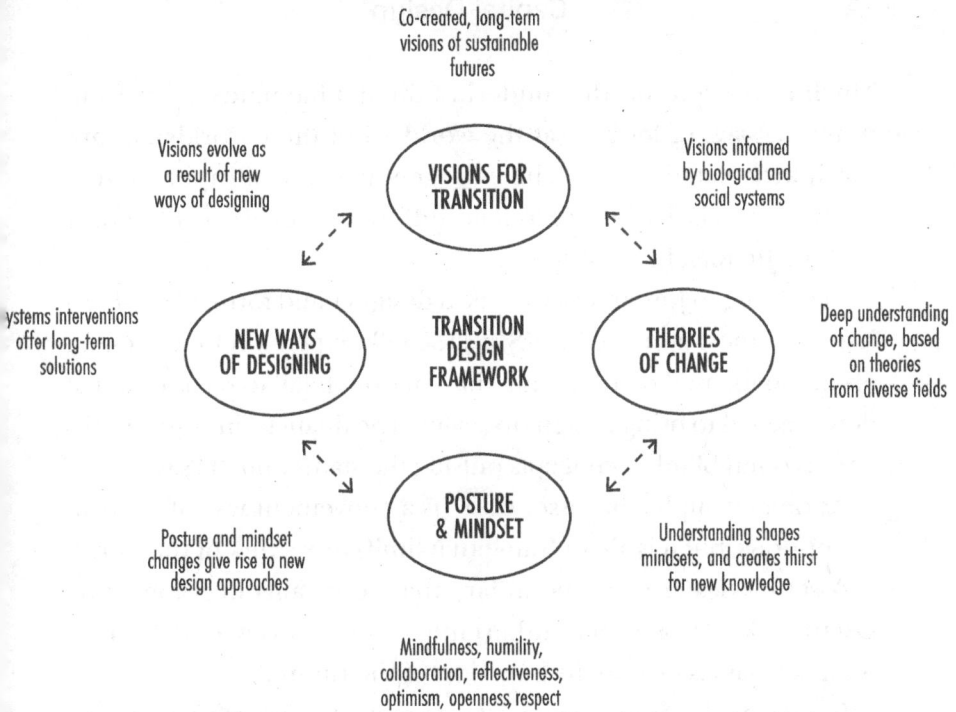

Figure 8.1 *An overview of transition design. (Irwin, 2015)*

communities, and the planet, and to take on the massive task of
reconceiving systems at a global level.

If this seems a tall order, it undoubtedly is – in large part
because of our society's attachment to extractive, financialized
epistemologies. But it can start simply enough, by seeking to
engage stakeholders through approaches like multi-stakeholder
governance, multi-stakeholder processes, stakeholder analysis,
and participatory action research. From there, collaborative
design approaches can help create new visions for the future,
pathways for change, and concrete designs from which we can
take action.

Capital Design

Much of the tension that underlies the double binds arises from different ways of looking at the world – but these worldviews are rarely articulated clearly. The emergent practice of capital design attempts to clarify and reconcile differences between designers and the financial industry.

According to Jordan Ostapchuk, a designer and former Vice-President of Innovation at OMERS, a $130 billion pension fund, designers are so focused on designing that they often fail to see the capital flows needed to bring designs to reality. The financial industry, for its part, is often blind to concepts outside the status quo, he says.

As one example, an "asset class" is a convenient way of narrowing options, but it is also a frame that limits one's view of the world.

Asset classes create a boundary that constrains decisions, says Ostapchuk: "An asset class inherently limits your view of the world. An asset class is essentially a version of the future."

It once made sense to use asset classes such as infrastructure, real estate, or private equity as a lens for design: A few decades ago, the infrastructure asset class meant a power plant or a toll road. But the world is changing faster than institutions' ability to conceptualize it; there are many gray areas, such as energy transition, that combine asset classes in ways not contemplated in the past.

Designers can bring fresh approaches and ways of seeing to investment decisions. As an example, an investment committee can relatively easily quantify the size of the EV charging market. Yet because it is unable to quantify millennial attitudes towards car ownership, it will omit information that could make or break the investment. "Even to bring it up, you sound a little bit crazy," says Ostapchuk.

Therein lies the opportunity for capital design. Designers can distill massive complexity into something workable, reframe it, and put it into context – and thereby ask provocative, and fundamental, questions: "What are we actually doing? What *should* we be doing? Are we trying to jam something in? Are we trying to make a decision and jam it into a preset set of choices?"

This does not mean designers have to abandon their value system to collaborate with the financial industry, or somehow to force the industry to see things their way, but instead, to use design methods like visualization and prototyping to make values explicit and clear.

Capital and design need each other, argues Ostapchuk. "For capitalism to continue to succeed, it has to be seen as delivering value – not just money, but making people's lives better ... If it's not doing that, it's failing."

If, however, design is the handmaiden of the tech sector and fails to bring its unique perspective to bear, it risks irrelevance. By contributing a designer's worldview to capital decisions, design can live up to its promise for transformative change.

Values remain central, and working in this way is not about abandoning values, but exposing them. "I think design should have a value set," says Ostapchuk, "and it should also force *everyone* to make their own value set explicit. Because ... you are making choices and decisions based on values, whether you know it or not."

Getting There

Our purpose in this book has been to show how designers and managers can work together to redesign value in the face of seemingly insurmountable and often invisible obstacles. Yet, as the examples in earlier chapters have shown, designers inside organizations are successfully overcoming these barriers daily. In Table 8.1, we summarize the double binds we identified, and the tactics some of the designers we spoke to are using to loosen them.

Table 8.1 *Summary of the double binds, and tactics for loosening them*

Bind	Description	Loosen by ...	Explanation
Workstyle Bind	Designers' ways of working disrupt corporate norms	Shifting mentality by doing	Demonstrate the difference and how/why it works
		Be explicit	Highlight the difference in mindset and output
		Solve their pain points	Find out their goals and show how design helps achieve them
Risk Bind	Organizations need to take risks, but balk at straying from status quo	Make things tangible	Make low-fidelity prototypes
		Model change from the top	Engage leaders in encouraging risk taking
		Use your empathy	Empathize with colleagues as you empathize with users
		Take a risk yourself	Model behavior to colleagues
Silo Bind	Silos and silo mentality obstruct design	Distribute design across silos	Place designers across the organization
		Create a collaborative team	Build design team from across corporate functions
		Manage around the user journey	Build design team according to user, not corporate needs
		Use stories	Tell user stories that show benefits of cross-silo work
		Combat your own silo mentality	Be easy to work with
Business Model Bind	Conflict between creating value and extracting value	Design the tradeoffs	Designers define how user value and business value are traded off
		Challenge the measures	Demonstrate the limits and bias of traditional data
		Bring in different perspectives	Use qualitative data, stories, and videos to broaden internal perspectives
Scope Bind	Design kept in a box, sealed off from anything important	Redesign the culture	Promote a design-centric culture
		Untying from the top down	Find a committed executive sponsor and expand
		Build legitimacy	Demonstrate design through use cases, not trivial exercises
		Take advantage of serendipity	Be alert for opportunities to demonstrate design's value
Epistemology Bind	Design conflicts with established ways of knowing	Choose work intentionally	Be up-front about values and intentional about work
		Find your people	Look inside and outside the organization for like-minded designers and managers
		Understand power dynamics	Map and discuss power

The reader can refer to the chapters on each bind for a more thorough discussion of these tactics. Each has been successful in its own context, but of course different contexts demand different approaches. Underlying these tactics, we see several broader principles that designers and managers would be wise to keep in mind.

Each principle is based on the experience of people working to bring about change, and to integrate social and environmental issues into their organizational culture. Think of them as guidelines for initiating conversations, and action, to redesign value.

Principle 1: Start with Relationships

If designers and managers are to create new forms of value together, they must start by changing how they interact with each other. Rather than go along with things – reinforcing existing dysfunctions – or reject the entire system, they must develop strong relationships, using design to transcend disciplinary boundaries. Says former OCADU Dean Dr. Dori Tunstall, "You need to understand how to connect with people. Engineers have the technology but don't know exactly what to build; businesspeople understand what can increase revenue or save cost – but it's the designer who makes it real. And even if that's all they expect, there's an added value: They're creating harmonious relationships."

"There's always pressure to move quickly and not spend time on things like relationships," said Eloise Smith-Foster, whom we met in the last chapter. "I was really inspired by the concept of 'fractals' by Adrienne Maree Brown," she told us. Brown's book *Emergent Strategy* has become a mainstay for activists. "A fractal is part of the larger system, where you can start to make change in a more manageable way. It starts with one relationship or one conversation." Rather than take on the daunting task of trying to change an entire system, Smith-Foster focuses on shifting individuals' mindsets. "It might feel quite small, but each interaction is a fractal of a bigger system. And that's how change can ripple out."

As designers feel the double bind of organizations espousing to create value for their customers while simultaneously working at every step to extract it, it's easy to become indignant. But as Sarah Drummond reminds us, designers must avoid becoming the jerk in the corner, by setting clear expectations and treating stakeholders as "a mate you can take for a beer and have real conversations with."

Principle 2: Design Materials *and* Mindsets

Designers can apply design practice not just to creating products, services, and experiences, but also to transforming their colleagues' mindsets. A particularly powerful approach is to engage their participation throughout a project. "We are including teams in collecting and analyzing research, to help with impact," says Kalle Petterson, senior policy designer at Experio Lab, a public service design lab in Sweden. "They're more understanding of citizens' perspective than [when] we [just] report back. When we do the research, it can feel less relevant and doesn't hit them in the stomach in the same way." Don't underestimate value in the process and consciously resource project engagements to redesign materials and mindsets simultaneously.

In organizations with entrenched beliefs and norms, designers can employ reflective activities such as Vink's iceberg model from chapter 6. By opening up discussions about seemingly fixed elements within organizations such as roles and norms, designers can expose mindsets and help them evolve. In doing this, they need to go beyond the standard journey maps and visual mockups, to address challenges shrouded deep within the organizational context.

Principle 3: Collectively Confront Assumptions

Designers and managers need to be constantly aware of the assumptions – especially those grounded in positivism, the illusion of objectivity, the extractive business model, financialization, and colonialism – that underlie the prevailing culture in their organization. At the same time – without compromising their own values – they must be humble and appreciate their own hidden assumptions and limitations. Financialization and efficiency are key parts of contemporary economies, and metrics have material impact on individual and organizational performance. As one manuscript reviewer for this book put it, designers may not get a seat at the table if "they treat profit as a moral failing."

One way to challenge assumptions is to elevate conversations beyond the immediate context. In the story of Sidewalk Labs in chapter 1, we saw how an unquestioning belief in technology's ability to solve civic problems led the company to overlook, or completely ignore, negative consequences on areas such as individual privacy.

Similarly, Sam Ladner, a sociologist and design researcher in the Bay Area, recalled how people in the tech community can believe they're in a privileged position to understand and solve every problem. "There are a lot of tech bros who think they alone have the answer to all of our problems," she said ruefully. By challenging the assumptions inherent in techno-solutionism, we can reflect on the negative unintended consequences and expand what's possible.

Principle 4: Kairos over Chronos

Kairos refers to the "right or critical moment," whereas chronos is simply defined as time.[8] For Greek philosopher Aristotle, Kairos held an important role as it indicated the time-and-space context in which the proof would be delivered. Understanding the role of timing and context is key to driving change.

As we noted in chapter 1, widely publicized incidents like the murder of George Floyd, the Canadian Truth and Reconciliation Commission's report on Indian Residential Schools, and the trial of Harvey Weinstein brought shifts in societal consciousness and a willingness to embrace change. We saw in previous chapters how designers like Peter Chow at RBC and Shannah Segal in the Ontario government leveraged the COVID-19 pandemic to demonstrate the value of design. In addition to a clear-eyed commitment to a better future, designers and managers need patience, persistence – and readiness for the right moment to make a compelling argument for redesigning value. As Hippocrates wrote "Every kairos is a chronos, but not every chronos is a kairos."[9]

Principle 5: Design's Way Forward

Redesigning value means not just talking about design, but showing that it can address major social and environmental challenges. We were particularly struck by our conversation with Jon Iwata, formerly IBM's chief brand officer and founder of the Yale Program on Stakeholder Innovation and Management. Because it shows how much can change when managers and designers work together, we discuss it here, as we bring our practical manifesto to a close.

Iwata discussed his experiences working with The Hartford Group, a Fortune 500 insurance company that committed to

become net zero by 2050. Key to the Hartford's Stakeholder Innovation program was applying the co-creation approach commonly
used by designers to identify the needs and perspectives of different
parties – not only users, but internal as well as external stakeholders.
"We incorporated the shareholder perspective, the employee perspective, and internal committees that are important to authorizing
any resource allocation authorization," he told us. From this starting point, the group could establish the appropriate constraints to
avoid implementation challenges and accelerate progress.

Iwata described how these approaches, along with others,
opened managers up to completely new opportunities to innovate
on the pressing challenge of reaching net zero, and on taking the
necessary steps to implement them. "They were thinking about
things like putting green roofs on their buildings, or carpooling
for employees," he said. "After the exercise, they began coalition
building to lead the creation of new regulations and changing
their core products and policies."

Iwata is passionate about making progress on social and environmental issues, and he sees design as a practical approach to driving
change. "Most of [the CEOs] say, "This is a new competitive reality.
You're not going to have a good business if you don't do more than
make money. People won't work for you. We can't just make great
products – people want to have more meaning in their work life."

Investors, too, are applying pressure like never before. "The big
institutional investors are asking us tough questions about DEI
and sustainability," continued Iwata. "They're pragmatic, and that
drives them to pay attention to things like values and purpose – to
make this authentic." Iwata credits his success on applying a design
approach. "[Design] gave us a common vocabulary that we did not
have, because each of us speaks a different business language."

"We're naïve enough to believe we can change the world and
bold enough to take the chance to do it," according to a recent

design job posting. If you read postings for design jobs in public and private sector organizations, you'll find plenty of aspirational statements like this. But too often, designers instead find themselves entangled in double binds, tasked with maintaining the status quo – reductive, extractive work that does nothing for society or the planet – not change.

What does it mean to redesign value? It means questioning *everything*: the ideas, assumptions, power structures, asset classes, project scope, and ways of thinking that got us to where we are. It means abandoning the relentless search for control and embracing ambiguity. It means making room for other ways of knowing and being. For optimism over cynicism, making over telling, humility over swagger, clear thinking over obscure jargon, mind of a child over mind of a robot.

And it means understanding that *both* managers and designers ultimately need the same thing: a more equitable, resilient economy and society. Yet all too often, instead of creating pathways to a better future, organizations tie designers up in double binds.

Can managers and designers work together to untie the binds and redesign our world? We remain confident that they can. It will take focused effort from designers, managers – and those educating the next generation – to build mutual respect and redefine what value means. It is no exaggeration to say that our collective future depends on it.

Notes

Chapter 1: Faking Design

1 https://www.thestar.com/news/city_hall/2017/06/28/toronto-waterfront
-receives-125-billion-to-clean-up-and-protect-the-port-lands.html.
2 https://www.ft.com/content/50bb4830-6a4c-11e6-ae5b-a7cc5dd5a28c.
3 https://www.cnet.com/tech/computing/mirror-mirror-show-me-my-vital-signs/.
4 https://www.cbc.ca/radio/thecurrent/the-current-for-june-25-2019-1.5188733
/sidewalk-labs-1-3b-plan-for-toronto-s-waterfront-is-bad-for-democracy-critic
-says-1.5188753. Accessed June 26, 2023.
5 O'Kane, J. (2022). *Sideways: The city Google couldn't buy*. Random House Canada.
6 https://techwontsave.us/episode/135_why_googles_toronto_smart_city_failed_w
_josh_okane.
7 O'Kane. *Sideways*.
8 Labarre, S. (2022). Why corporate America broke up with design. *Fast Company*
October 5. https://www.fastcompany.com/90779666/why-corporate-america
-broke-up-with-design.
9 In this book, we use the term "designer" broadly. It is not restricted to people who
have gone to design school but includes anyone committed to the idea of design or
design thinking as an approach to problem solving, value creation, and innovation.
10 Though the main focus of this book is on private-sector business, design has
been widely adopted in the public and not-for-profit sectors too. In these sectors,
the drive for efficiency, and hostile organizational cultures, lead to similar
dysfunction to the private sector.
11 Carnegie, A. (2011). *The autobiography of Andrew Carnegie*. Public Affairs. First
published 1920.
12 Carnegie, A. (1906). The gospel of wealth. *The North American Review, 183*(599),
526–37.

13 Braverman, H. (1974). *Labor and monopoly capital: The degradation of work in the twentieth century*. Monthly Review Press.
14 Friedman, M. (1970). A Friedman doctrine: The social responsibility of business is to increase its profits. *The New York Times Magazine* 13, no. 1970: 32–3.
15 Handy, C. (2002). What's a business for? *Harvard Business Review*, November–December.
16 Porter, M.E., & Kramer, M.R. (2011). Creating shared value: Redefining capitalism and the role of the corporation in society. *Harvard Business Review*, *89*(1/2): 62–77.
17 Porter, Michael E., Kramer, Mark R., Herman, Kerry, and McCara, Sara. (2017). Nestlé's creating shared value strategy. Case # 9-716-422. *Harvard Business School Publishing*.
18 Nestlé Canada. Creating shared value: Our purpose in action 2021/2022. https://ca.factory.nestle.com/sites/g/files/pydnoa556/files/2022-08/2021%20 2022%20Nestle%20CSV%20Snapshot%20-%20ENG.pdf.
19 https://opportunity.businessroundtable.org/ourcommitment/.
20 Bell, Brian, & Van Reenen, J. (2014). Bankers and their bonuses. *The Economic Journal* 124, no. 574: F1–F21.
21 Treanor, Jill. (October 13, 2015). Half of world's wealth now in hands of 1% of population – report. *The Guardian*.
22 Who exactly are the 1%? The very rich in America increasingly work in finance, marry each other, and care passionately about politics. (January 21, 2012), *The Economist*.
23 Tugend, A. (2013). The Guilty Age. *Worth Magazine*, April 7. https://worth.com /the-guilty-age/.
24 Previously posted on wealthforthecommongood.org (site no longer available).
25 Piketty, T. (2013). *Capital in the 21st century*. Cambridge, MA: President and Fellows, Harvard College.
26 Fagan, M., & Huang, C. (2019). A look at how people around the world view climate change. Pew Research Center. https://www.pewresearch.org/fact -tank/2019/04/18/a-look-at-how-people-around-the-world-view-climate-change/.
27 Porter, M.E., & Rinehart, F.L. (2007). Grist: A Strategic Approach to Climate. *Harvard Business Review*, October.
28 Bristow, S. (June 2007). Business and climate change: Rising public awareness creates significant opportunity. *UN Chronicle*, XLIV, 2, Green Our World! https://www.un.org/en/chronicle/article/business-and-climate-change-rising -public-awareness-creates-significant-opportunity.
29 Wolf, M. (2023). The crisis of democratic capitalism. Penguin Press.
30 Leavy, B. (2020). Roger Martin: The problematic economic efficiency mindset that threatens corporations and democratic society. *Strategy & Leadership*, *48*(6), 3–9. https://doi.org/10.1108/SL-07-2020-0107.
31 The term "residential schools" refers to an extensive school system set up by the Canadian government and administered by churches that had the nominal objective of educating Indigenous children, but also the more damaging and equally explicit objectives of indoctrinating them into Euro-Canadian and Christian ways of living and assimilating them into mainstream white Canadian society. (https://indigenousfoundations.arts.ubc.ca/the_residential_school_system/.)
32 Schumpeter. (2013, July 6). Back to the drawing-board: Design companies are applying their skills to the voluntary and public sectors. *The Economist*.

33 Simon, H.A. (2019). *The Sciences of the Artificial,* reissue of the third edition with a new introduction by John Laird. MIT press.
34 Cross, N. (2001). Designerly ways of knowing: Design discipline versus design science. *Design Issues, 17*(3), 49–55.
35 Elsbach, K.D., & Stigliani, I. (2018). Design thinking and organizational culture: A review and framework for future research. *Journal of Management, 44*(6), 2274–306.
36 Skaburskis, A. (2008). The origin of "wicked problems." *Planning Theory & Practice, 9*(2), 277–80.
37 Rittel, H.W., & Webber, M.M. (1973). Dilemmas in a general theory of planning. *Policy sciences, 4*(2), 155–69.
38 Jones, J.C. (1977). How my thoughts about design methods have changed during the years. *Design Methods and Theories,* 11, 1.
39 Schön, D.A. (2017). *The reflective practitioner: How professionals think in action.* Routledge.
40 Apple "1984" commercial, aired January 23, 1984. Directed by Ridley Scott, written by Steve Hayden, produced by Fairbanks Films.
41 https://www.smithsonianmag.com/arts-culture/how-steve-jobs-love-of-simplicity-fueled-a-design-revolution-23868877/.
42 Dunne, D. (2013). User-centred design and design-centred business schools. In R. Cooper, S. Junginger, & T. Lockwood (Eds.), *The handbook of design management* (pp. 128–143). A&C Black.
43 Norman, D.A. (1988). *The design of everyday things.* Basic books. Originally titled "The psychology of everyday things."
44 Buchanan, R. (1992). Wicked problems in design thinking. *Design issues, 8*(2), 5–21.
45 Buchanan, R. (2001). Design research and new learning. Design issues, *17*(4), 3–23.
46 Buchanan, R. (2001). "Design Research and the New Learning." *Design Issues, 17*(4) (Autumn): 3–23.
47 Liu, A.X., & de Bont, C. (2017). Barriers to strategic design: A perspective from China. *She Ji: The Journal of Design, Economics, and Innovation, 3*(2), 117–32.
48 https://designthinking.ideo.com/.
49 Martin, R.L. (2009). *The design of business: Why design thinking is the next competitive advantage.* Harvard Business Press.
50 Boland, R., & Collopy, F. (Eds.). (2004). *Managing as designing.* Stanford Business Books.
51 In this book, we generally avoid the use of the term "design thinking" because it has become so misleading, except where we are referring to its adoption in business and government. For further discussion, see Badke-Schaub, P., Roozenburg, N., & Cardoso, C. (2010, October). Design thinking: A paradigm on its way from dilution to meaninglessness. In *Proceedings of the 8th Design Thinking Research Symposium* (DTRS8) (pp. 39–49). Sydney: DAB documents.
52 Bateson, G. (1972). *Steps to an ecology of mind: Collected essays in anthropology, psychiatry, evolution, and epistemology.* University of Chicago Press.
53 Carr, A. (2015). The evolution of systems theory. In *Handbook of family therapy* (pp. 13–29). Routledge.
54 Lockton, D. (2018). Old rope: Laing's knots and Bateson's double binds in systemic design. In *Proceedings of RSD7, Relating Systems Thinking and Design 7,* 23–6 Oct. 2018, Turin, Italy. Available at http://openresearch.ocadu.ca/id/eprint/2744/.

Chapter 2: The Workstyle Bind

1 https://rework.withgoogle.com/print/guides/5721312655835136/.
2 https://www.nytimes.com/2016/02/28/magazine/what-google-learned-from-its -quest-to-build-the-perfect-team.html. Accessed June 13, 2023.
3 https://www.scientificamerican.com/article/what-is-the-memory-capacity/.
4 https://thebrain.mcgill.ca/flash/capsules/experience_jaune03.html.
5 Brown, T. (2019). *Change by design: How design thinking transforms organizations and inspires innovation*. HarperCollins.
6 Martin, R.L. (2009). *The design of business: Why design thinking is the next competitive advantage*. Harvard Business Press.
7 https://www.youtube.com/watch?v=D3qr1EXs2sA. Accessed June 14, 2023.
8 Kolko, J. (2010). *Thoughts on interaction design*. Morgan Kaufmann.
9 https://www.sciencedirect.com/topics/computer-science/epistemic-action. Accessed June 14, 2023.

Chapter 3: The Risk Bind

1 http://www.altfuels.org/misc/onlygm.pdf. Accessed May 22, 2023.
2 Paine, C. (Director & Writer). (2006). Who killed the electric car. Electric Entertainment.
3 https://www.reuters.com/graphics/AUTOS-INVESTMENT/ELECTRIC /akpeqgzqypr/. Accessed May 22, 2023.
4 Johnson, Peter. (2023, Jan 20). Why is GM investing nearly $1B in V-8 engines when it's "all in" on electric vehicles? *Electrek*. https://electrek.co/2023/01/20 /why-is-gm-investing-1b-in-v-8-engines-when-its-all-in-on-evs/.
5 Kuhn, T.S. (2012). *The structure of scientific revolutions*. University of Chicago Press.
6 https://www.hofstede-insights.com/.
7 The study measured "entrepreneurial orientation" using three variables: innovativeness, proactiveness, and risk-taking. Risk-taking is used as a shorthand here, since the results were identical between the three variables.
8 Humans Wanted: How Canadian youth can thrive in the age of disruption. RBC. https://www.rbc.com/dms/enterprise/futurelaunch/_assets-custom/pdf/RBC -Future-Skills-Report-FINAL-Singles.pdf. Accessed May 22, 2023.
9 Smulders, F., & Dunne, D. (2017). Disciplina: A missing link for cross-disciplinary integration. In *Analyzing Design Thinking: Studies of Cross-Cultural Co-Creation* (pp. 137–52). CRC Press.
10 https://www.discovermagazine.com/health/these-five-doctors-experimented-on -themselves-and-made-big-breakthroughs.

Chapter 4: The Silo Bind

1 Molek, N., de Jager, J.E., & Pucelj, M. (2023). Hero culture and silo mentality: A systematic literature review. *RUO. Revija za Univerzalno Odlicnost, 12*(1), 1–17.
2 Leavitt, H.J., & Kaufman, R. (2003). Why hierarchies thrive. *Harvard Business Review, 81*(3), 96–112.
3 Khan, S. (2015). When does equality flourish? *New Yorker*, June 5.
4 Mintzberg, H. (1989). *The structuring of organizations* (pp. 322–52). Macmillan Education UK.

5 Graeber, D., & Wengrow, D. (2021). *The dawn of everything: A new history of humanity* (First American edition.). Farrar, Straus and Giroux.
6 Vargo, S.L., & Lusch, R.F. (2004). Evolving to a new dominant logic for marketing. *Journal of Marketing*, 68(1), 1–17M.
7 Prahalad, C.K., & Ramaswamy, V. (2004). *The future of competition: Co-creating unique value with customers.* Harvard Business Press.
8 Prahalad, C.K., & Ramaswamy, V. (2004). Co-creation experiences: The next practice in value creation. *Journal of Interactive Marketing, 18*(3), 5–14.
9 Porter, M.E. (1980). *Competitive strategy: Techniques for analyzing industries and competitors.* The Free Press.
10 Diamond, M.A., & Allcorn, S. (2009). Silo mentality. In *Private selves in public organizations: The psychodynamics of organizational diagnosis and change* (49–72). New York: Palgrave Macmillan.
11 Tausk, V. (1919). On the origin of the "influencing machine" in schizophrenia. In R. Fliess (Ed.), *The Psychoanalytic Reader* (pp. 31–64). New York: International Universities Press.
12 Tausk, V. (1919). On the origin of the "influencing machine."
13 Tarling, Kate. (2023). *The service organization* (113) London Publishing Partnership.

Chapter 5: The Business Model Bind

1 https://www.ibm.com/ibm/history/ibm100/us/en/icons/gooddesign/.
2 Boland, R., & Collopy, F. (Eds.). (2004). *Managing as designing* (p. 298). Stanford Business Books.
3 https://www.fastcompany.com/90779666/why-corporate-america-broke-up-with-design. Accessed June 6, 2023.
4 https://www.mckinsey.com/capabilities/mckinsey-design/our-insights/the-business-value-of-design. Accessed June 6, 2023.
5 https://www.mckinsey.com/capabilities/mckinsey-design/how-we-help-clients/design-blog/how-design-helps-incumbents-build-new-businesses. Accessed June 7, 2023.
6 https://www150.statcan.gc.ca/n1/daily-quotidien/220803/dq220803a-eng.htm.
7 https://www.globenewswire.com/news-release/2022/05/18/2445753/0/en/Workplace-Study-Canadian-workers-more-dissatisfied-than-ever.html.
8 Vargo, S.L., & Lusch, R.F. (2004). Evolving to a new dominant logic for marketing. *Journal of Marketing, 68*(1), 1–17.
9 Pine, B.J., & Gilmore, J.H. (2011). *The experience economy.* Harvard Business Press.

Chapter 6: The Scope Bind

1 Dunne, D. (2023). Throwing a hand grenade at the bureaucracy – MindLab and wicked problems in government. In J. Schweitzer, S. BenMahmoud-Jouini, and Sebastian Fixson (Eds.), *Transform with design: Creating new innovation capabilities with design thinking.* University of Toronto Press.
2 Carstensen, H.V., & Bason, C. (2012). Powering collaborative policy innovation: Can innovation labs help? *The Innovation Journal: The Public Sector Innovation Journal 17*(1), 1–26.
3 Costanza-Chock, S. (2020). *Design justice: Community-led practices to build the worlds we need.* (122–3), The MIT Press.

4 Conklin, J. (2006). *Wicked problems & social complexity* (Vol. 11). CogNexus Institute.
5 Few, J.A. (2015). How Indra Nooyi turned design thinking into strategy. *Harvard Business Review*, 2015, 80–5.
6 Vink. (2019). In/Visible – shaping hidden social structures through service design. Presentation, Service Design Network, Toronto. https://www.youtube.com/watch?v=JCfK03drxbA.
7 Pirsig, R.M. (1999). *Zen and the art of motorcycle maintenance: An inquiry into values.* Random House.
8 Gilley, A., Godek, M., & Gilley, J.W. (2009). Change, resistance, and the organizational immune system. *SAM Advanced Management Journal 74*(4), 4.
9 Jeanne Liedtka on the "Moses Myth" of innovation. Columbia University Press blog. https://cupblog.org/2013/10/02/lietdka-the-moses-myth-of-innovation/.
10 Vink, J., Edvardsson, B., Wetter-Edman, K., & Tronvoll, B. (2019). Reshaping mental models – enabling innovation through service design. *Journal of Service Management 30*(1), 75–104.
11 Lohr, Steve (2015. IBM's design-centered strategy to set free the squares. *New York Times*, Nov 14.
12 Rauth, I., Carlgren, L., & Elmquist, M. (2014). Making it happen: Legitimizing design thinking in large organizations. *Design Management Journal, 9*(1), 47–60.

Chapter 7: The Epistemology Bind

1 Robinson, M.D. (2019). Financializing epistemic norms in contemporary biomedical innovation. *Synthese (Dordrecht), 196*(11), 4391–407. https://doi.org/10.1007/s11229-018-1704-0.
2 Holman, B. (2019). Philosophers on drugs. *Synthese, 196*, 4363–390. https://doi.org/10.1007/s11229-017-1642-2.
3 https://www.nytimes.com/interactive/2023/06/08/upshot/new-york-city-smoke.html.
4 King, C. (2019). *Gods of the upper air: How a circle of renegade anthropologists reinvented race, sex, and gender in the twentieth century* (First edition.). Doubleday.
5 Bowker and Star, (2000). Sorting things out: Classification and its consequences. The MIT Press.
6 Battiste, M. (2017). Cognitive Imperialism. In Peters, M.A. (Ed.), *Encyclopedia of Educational Philosophy and Theory.* Springer, Singapore. https://doi.org/10.1007/978-981-287-588-4_501.
7 Shiva, V. (1993). *Monocultures of the Mind.* Trumpeter Research Foundation for Science.
8 Pronin, E., Lin, D.Y., & Ross, L. (2002). The Bias Blind Spot: Perceptions of Bias in Self Versus Others. *Personality and Social Psychology Bulletin, 28*(3), 369–381. https://doi.org/10.1177/0146167202286008
9 https://www.mckinsey.com/capabilities/mckinsey-digital/our-insights/the-creative-process-is-fabulously-unpredictable-a-great-idea-cannot-be-predicted. Accessed June 12, 2023.
10 Lazonick, W. (2010). Innovative business models and varieties of capitalism: Financialization of the U.S. corporation. *Business History Review, 84*(4), 675–702. https://doi.org/10.1017/S0007680500001987.

11 Vollmers, G. (2003). Industrial slavery in the United States: The North Carolina turpentine industry 1849–61. *Accounting, Business & Financial History, 13*(3), 369–92. https://doi.org/10.1080/09585200310001606626.
12 Pinto, O., & West, B. (2017). Accounting, slavery, and social history: The legacy of an eighteenth-century Portuguese chartered company. *Accounting History, 22*(2), 141–66. https://doi-org.myaccess.library.utoronto.ca/10.1177/1032373217696512.
13 Palley, T.I. (2013). *Financialization.* Springer Nature.
14 Mazzucato, Mariana, (2018). *The value of everything: Making and taking in the global economy.* PublicAffairs.
15 Mazzucato, M. (2021). *Mission economy: A moonshot guide to changing capitalism.* Allen Lane, an imprint of Penguin Books.
16 Carney, M. (2021). *Value(s): Building a better world for all.* William Collins.
17 https://hbr.org/2022/03/an-inconvenient-truth-about-esg-investing.
18 Keeley, T. (2022). *Sustainable: Moving beyond ESG to impact investing.* Columbia University Press.
19 Berg, F., Kölbel, J.F., & Rigobon, R. (2022). Aggregate confusion: The divergence of ESG ratings. *Review of Finance, 26*(6), 1315–44. https://doi.org/10.1093/rof/rfac033.
20 https://www.sustainability.com/thinking/rating-the-raters-yet-again-six-challenges-for-esg-ratings/.
21 Schiffer, E. (2007). The power mapping tool: A method for the empirical research of power relations, working paper. https://ageconsearch.umn.edu/record/42410/?v=pdf.

Chapter 8: Value, Redesigned

1 Nussbaum, B. (2011, Apr. 5). Design thinking is a failed experiment. So what's next? *Co.Design.* https://www.fastcodesign.com/1663558/design-thinking-is-a-failed-experiment-so-whats-next.
2 Kolko, J. (2018). The divisiveness of design thinking. *interactions, 25*(3), 28–34.
3 Vink, J., & Koskela-Huotari, K. (2022). Building reflexivity using service design methods. *Journal of Service Research, 25*(3), 371–89. https://doi.org/10.1177/10946705211035004.
4 Schwab, K., & Davis, N. (2018). Shaping the fourth industrial revolution. *World Economic Forum.*
5 https://www.weforum.org/focus/fourth-industrial-revolution/.
6 LinkedIn.com, posted by Robert Fabricant in April 2024.
7 Mazzucato, M. (2024, May 30). The ugly truth behind ChatGPT: AI is guzzling resources at planet-eating rates. *The Guardian.* https://www.theguardian.com/commentisfree/article/2024/may/30/ugly-truth-ai-chatgpt-guzzling-resources-environment.
8 Liddell and Scott, *Greek-English Lexicon.*
9 Sipiora, P., & Baumlin, J.S. (2002). *Rhetoric and Kairos: Essays in history, theory, and praxis* (pp. 97–9). State University of New York Press.

Index